SATB AND PIANO

AARON COPLAND

Old American Songs Complete

Contents

FIRST SET

SECOND SET

7777 W. Bluemound Rd. P.O. Box 13819 Milwaukee, WI 53213

www.boosey.com
www.halleonard.com

The first set of *Old American Songs* was completed in 1950, the same year that Copland finished his other major song set, *Twelve Poems of Emily Dickinson*. While Copland was writing the songs, tenor Peter Pears and composer Benjamin Britten came to visit him. Taken by Copland's new settings, they left with his promise of receiving copies of the songs in England to perform. On October 17, 1950, the first set was given its world premiere by Pears with Britten at the piano at their Aldeburgh Festival. The American premiere took place in New York on January 28, 1951, with Copland accompanying baritone William Warfield. The success of the first set prompted Copland to set five more songs. Finished in 1952, the second set was premiered by Warfield and Copland at the Castle Hill Concerts in Massachusetts on July 24 of that year. Copland would later orchestrate both sets for medium voice and small orchestra. Warfield sang the premiere of the orchestrated first set with the Los Angeles Philharmonic, conducted by Alfred Wallenstein, on January 7, 1955. Grace Bumbry premiered the second set with the Ojai Festival Orchestra on May 25, 1955, with Copland on the podium.

FIRST SET

1. *The Boatmen's Dance*
   Published in Boston in 1843 as an "original banjo melody" by Old Dan. D. Emmett, who later composed Dixie. From the Harris Collection of American Poetry and Plays in Brown University.

2. *The Dodger*
   As sung by Mrs. Emma Dusenberry of Mena, Arkansas, who learned it in the 1880's. Supposedly used in the Cleveland-Blaine presidential campaign. Published by John A. and Alan Lomax in *Our Singing Country*.

3. *Long Time Ago*
   Issued in 1837 by George Pope Morris, who adapted the words, and Charles Edward Horn, who arranged the music from an anonymous, original minstrel tune. Also from the Harris Collection.

4. *Simple Gifts*
   A favorite song of the Shaker sect, from the period 1837-1847. The melody and words were quoted by Edward D. Andrews in his book of Shaker rituals, songs and dances, entitled *The Gift To Be Simple*.

5. *I Bought Me a Cat*
   A children's nonsense song. This version was sung to the composer by the American playwright Lynn Riggs, who learned it during his boyhood in Oklahoma.

SECOND SET

1. *The Little Horses*
   A children's lullaby song originating in the Southern States – date unknown. This adaptation founded in part on John A. and Alan Lomax's version in *Folk Song U.S.A.*

2. *Zion's Walls*
   A revivalist song. Original melody and words credited to John G. McCurry, compiler of the *Social Harp*. Published by George P. Jackson in *Down East Spirituals.*

3. *The Golden Willow Tree*
   Variant of the well-known Anglo-American ballad, more usually called *The Golden Vanity*. This version is based on a recording issued by the Library of Congress Music Division from its collection of the Archive of American Folk Song. Justus Begley recorded it with banjo accompaniment for Alan and Elizabeth Lomax in 1937.

4. *At the River*
   Hymn Tune. Words and melody are by Rev. Robert Lowry, 1865.

5. *Ching-a-ring Chaw*
   Minstrel Song. The words have been adapted from the original, in the Harris Collection of American Poetry and Plays in Brown University.

First Set

1. THE BOATMEN'S DANCE

(Minstrel Song - 1843)

Arranged by
AARON COPLAND
Transcribed for chorus by
IRVING FINE

* For SATB with Baritone Solo.

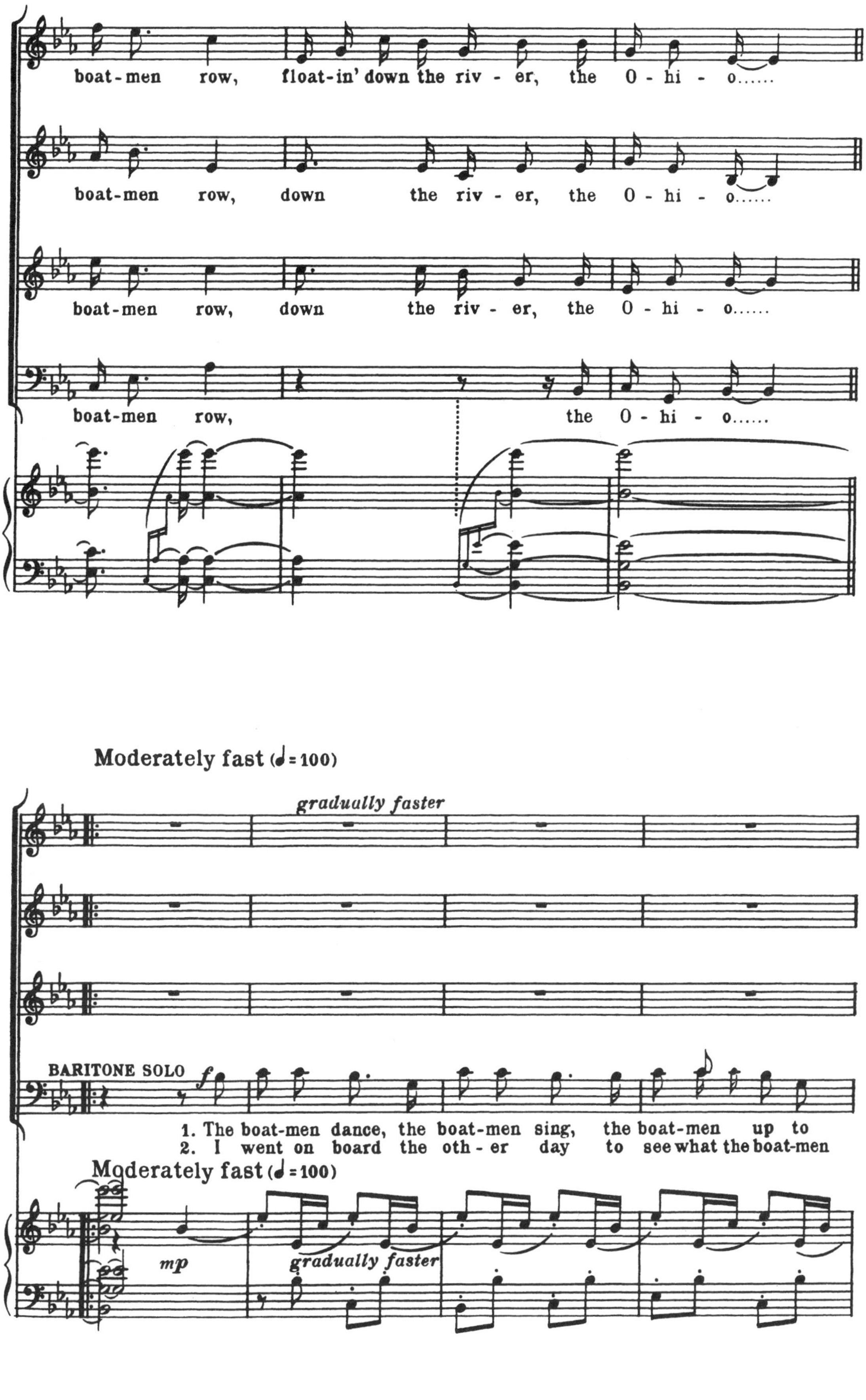

boat-men row, float-in' down the riv - er, the O - hi - o......

boat-men row, down the riv - er, the O - hi - o......

boat-men row, down the riv - er, the O - hi - o......

boat-men row, the O - hi - o......

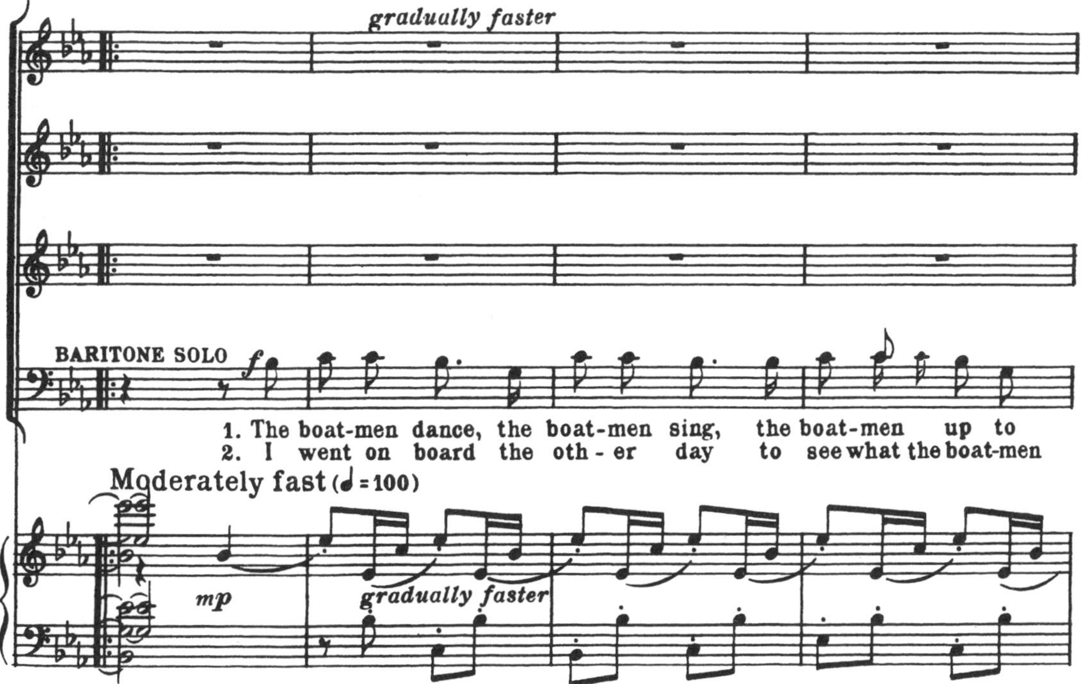

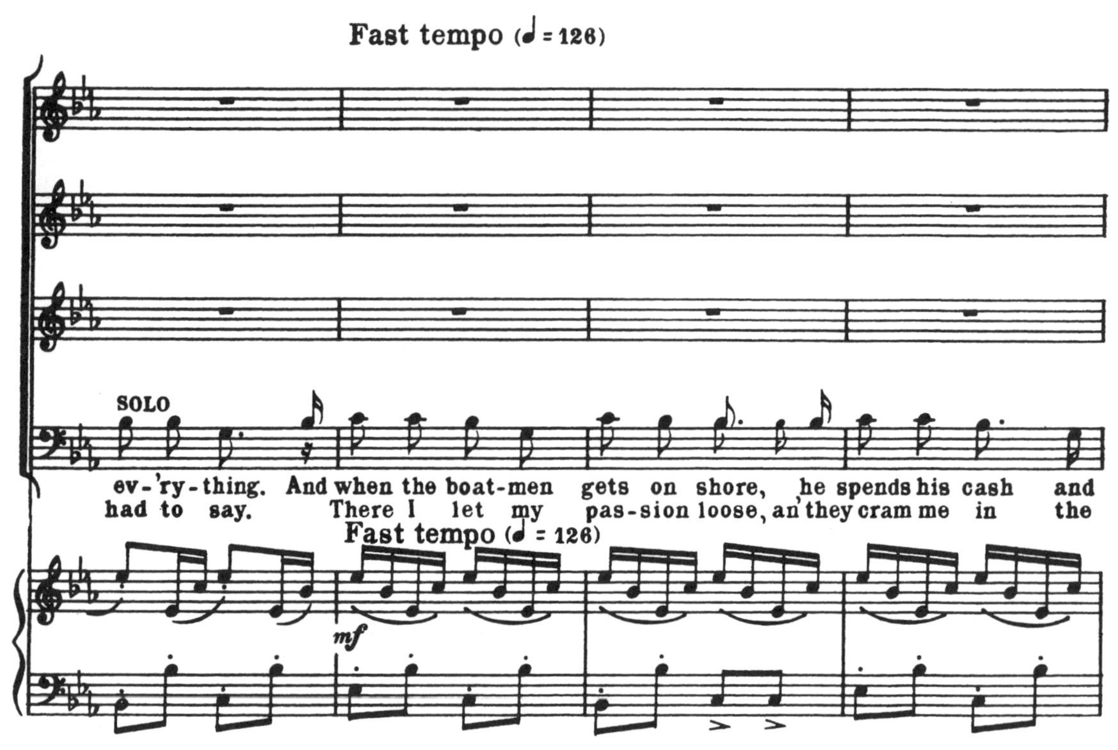

Fast tempo (♩ = 126)
SOLO
ev-'ry-thing. And when the boat-men gets on shore, he spends his cash and
had to say. There I let my pas-sion loose, an' they cram me in the
Fast tempo (♩ = 126)
mf

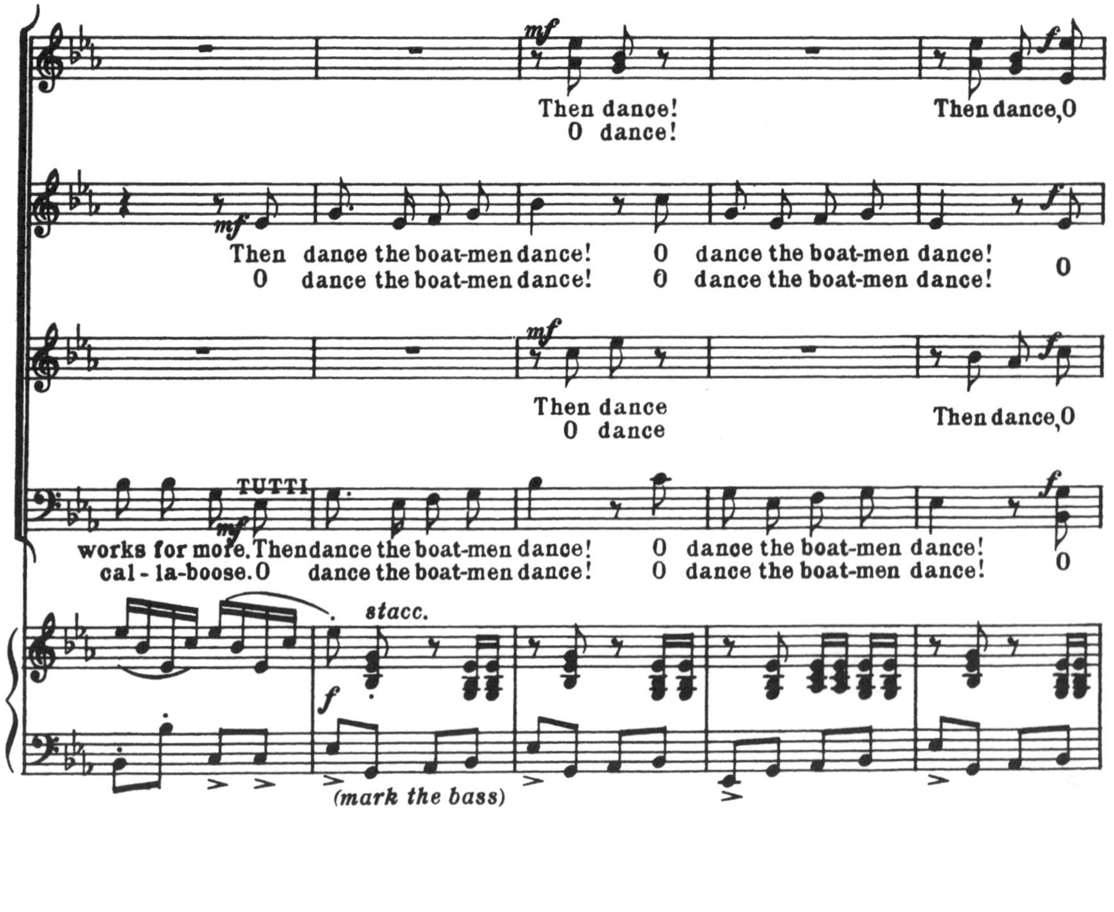
mf
Then dance!
O dance!
Then dance, O
mf
Then dance the boat-men dance! O dance the boat-men dance!
O dance the boat-men dance! O dance the boat-men dance!
O
f
Then dance
O dance
Then dance, O
TUTTI
works for more. Then dance the boat-men dance! O dance the boat-men dance!
cal-la-boose. O dance the boat-men dance! O dance the boat-men dance!
O
stacc.
f
(mark the bass)

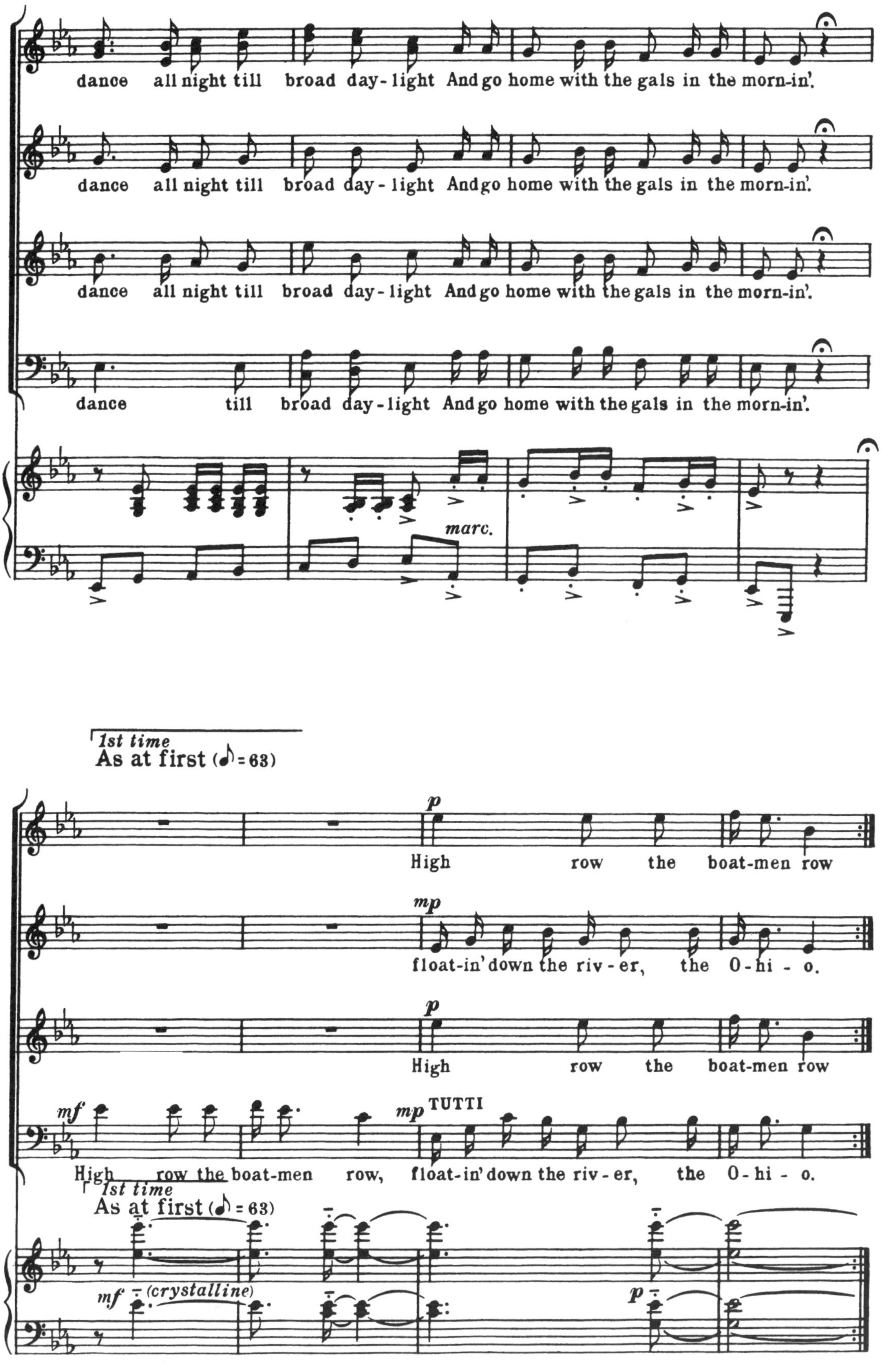

dance all night till broad day-light And go home with the gals in the morn-in'.

dance all night till broad day-light And go home with the gals in the morn-in'.

dance all night till broad day-light And go home with the gals in the morn-in'.

dance till broad day-light And go home with the gals in the morn-in'.

marc.

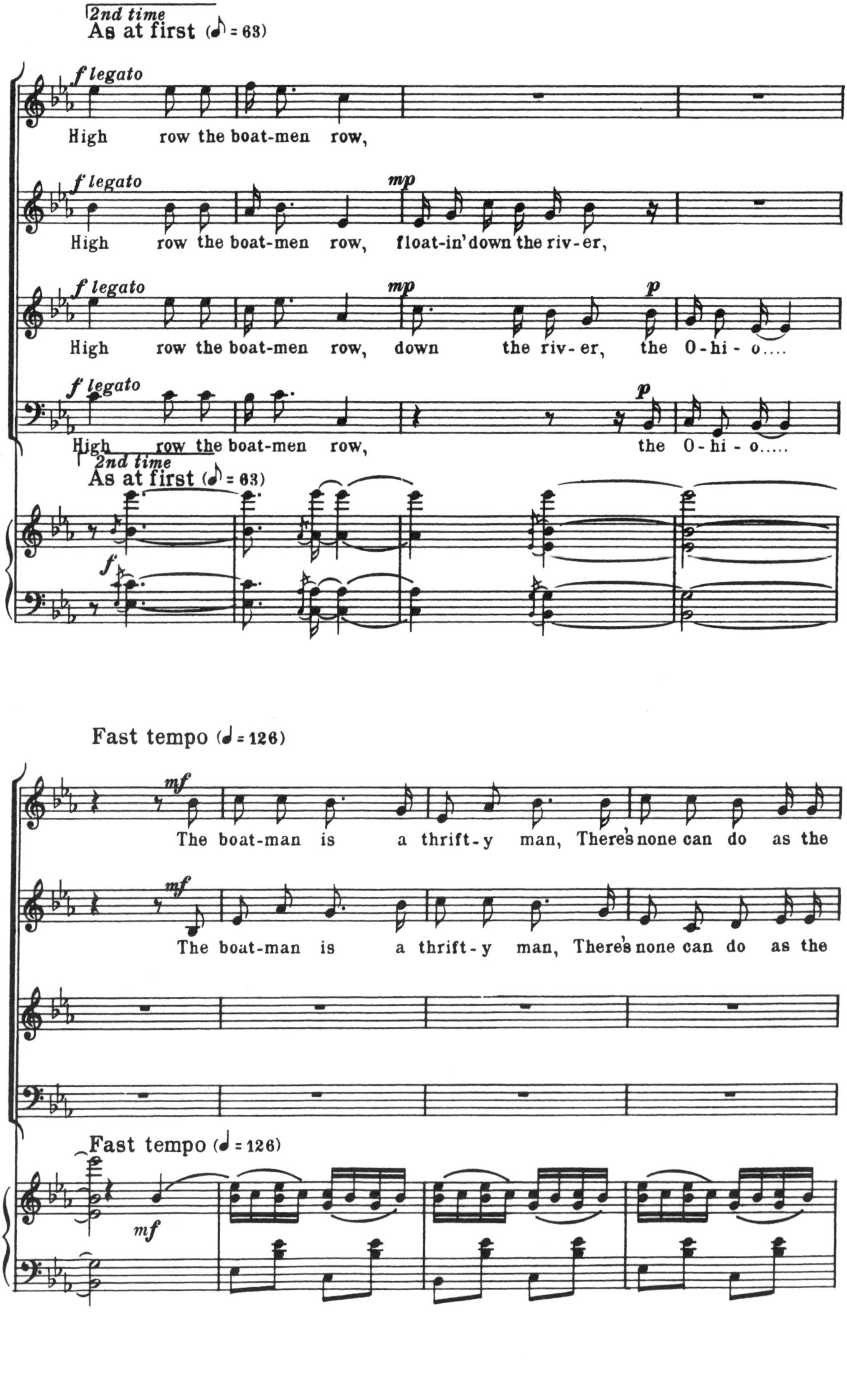

2nd time
As at first (♪ = 63)

f legato
High row the boat-men row,

f legato *mp*
High row the boat-men row, float-in' down the riv-er,

f legato *mp* *p*
High row the boat-men row, down the riv-er, the O-hi-o....

f legato *p*
High row the boat-men row, the O-hi-o.....

2nd time
As at first (♪ = 63)

f

boat - men can.
boat - men can. loo loo loo loo
I nev-er see a pret-ty girl in my life, But
that she was a boat-man's wife. O dance the boat-men dance! O
O dance the boat-men dance! O
that she was a boat-man's wife. O dance........................ Then dance! O
O dance the boat-men, Then dance! O
stacc.
(mark the bass)

dance the boat-men dance! O dance all night 'till broad day-light and go
dance the boat-men dance! O dance all night 'till broad day-light and go
dance,...................... Then dance! O dance all night 'till broad day-light and go
dance the boat-men, Then dance! O dance 'till broad day-light and go
marc.
As at first (♩ = 63)
home with the gals in the morn-in'!
home with the gals in the morn-in'!
home with the gals in the morn-in'!
home with the gals in the morn-in'! High row the boat-men row,
ff
As at first (♩ = 63)
ff
f

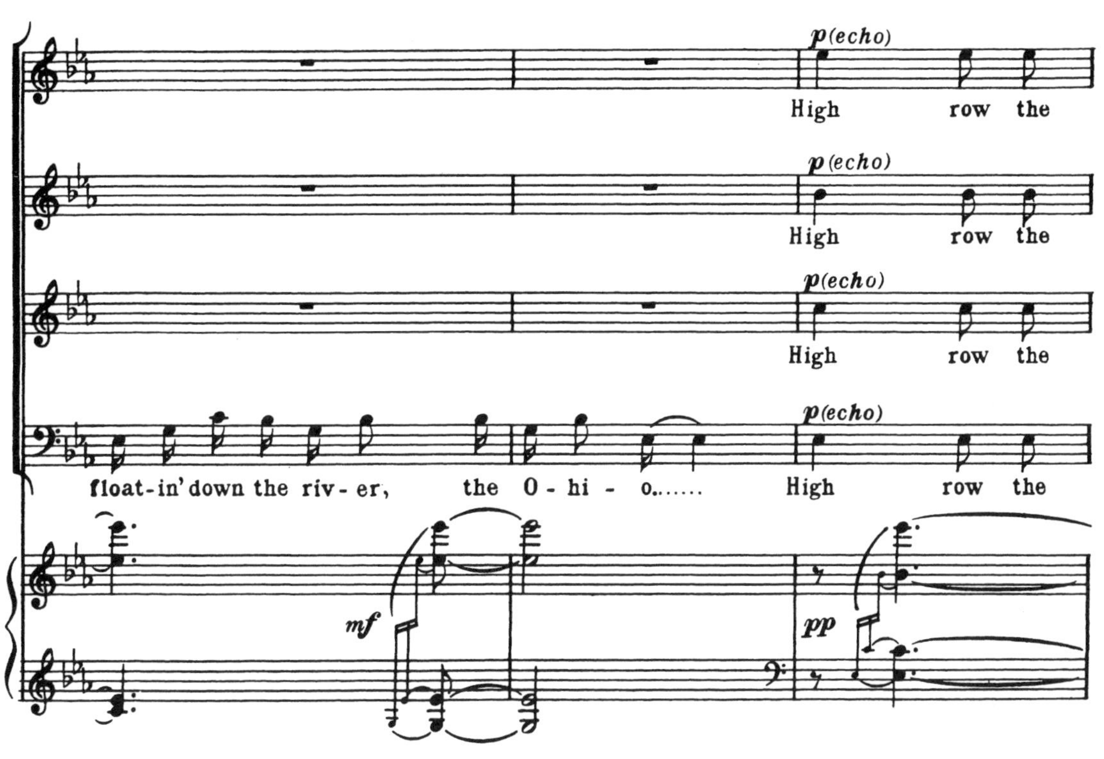
p(echo)
High row the
p(echo)
High row the
p(echo)
High row the
p(echo)
float-in' down the riv-er, the O-hi-o...... High row the
mf
pp

boat-men row, float in' down the riv-er, the O-hi-o.
boat-men row, down the riv-er, the O-hi-o.
boat-men row, down the riv-er, the O-hi-o-oo.
boat-men row, the O-hi-o-oo.
p

2. THE DODGER

(Campaign Song)

Arranged by
AARON COPLAND
Transcribed for chorus by
DAVID L. BRUNNER

9
f
can - di-date's a dodg - er, yes a well known dodg - er, Yes the
(mark the bass)

11
can - di-date's a dodg - er, yes and I'm a dodg - er too

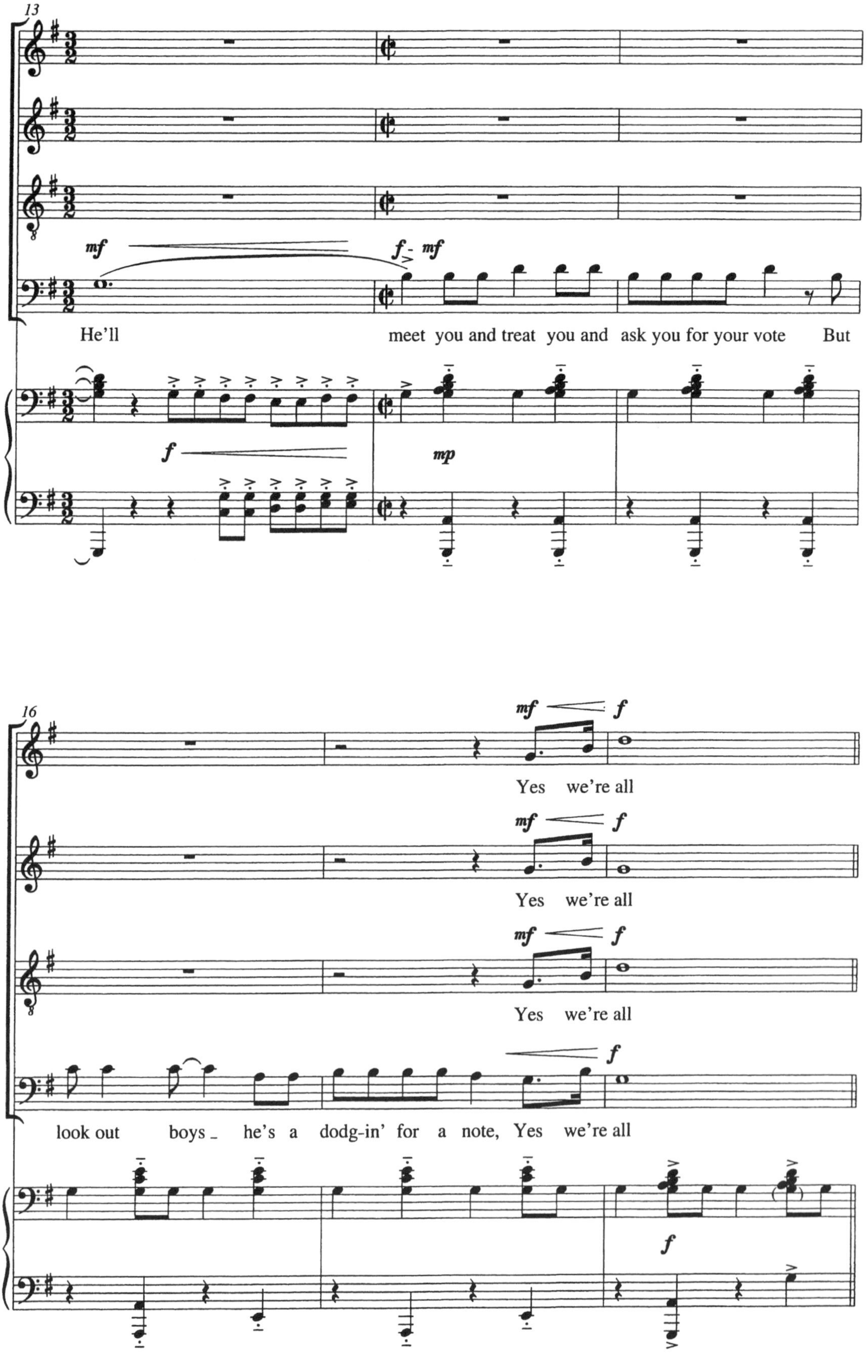

16

mf *f*

Yes we're all

mf *f*

Yes we're all

mf *f*

Yes we're all

f

look out boys _ he's a dodg-in' for a note, Yes we're all

f

19

ff

dodg - in' ___ a - dodg - in', dodg - in', dodg - in' Yes we're all

ff

dodg - in' ___ a - dodg - in', dodg - in', dodg - in' Yes we're all

ff

dodg - in' ___ a - dodg - in', dodg - in', dodg - in' Yes we're all

ff

dodg - in' ___ a - dodg - in', dodg - in', dodg - in' Yes we're all

23

dodg - in' out a way through the world ___

dodg - in' out a way through the world ___

dodg - in' out a way through the world ___

dodg - in' out a way through the world ___

ff

sf sf sf

27
2nd time only mp
Yes
2nd time only mp
Yes
1st time only mp
Yes
sf
sf
sf
sf
sf
sf
sf

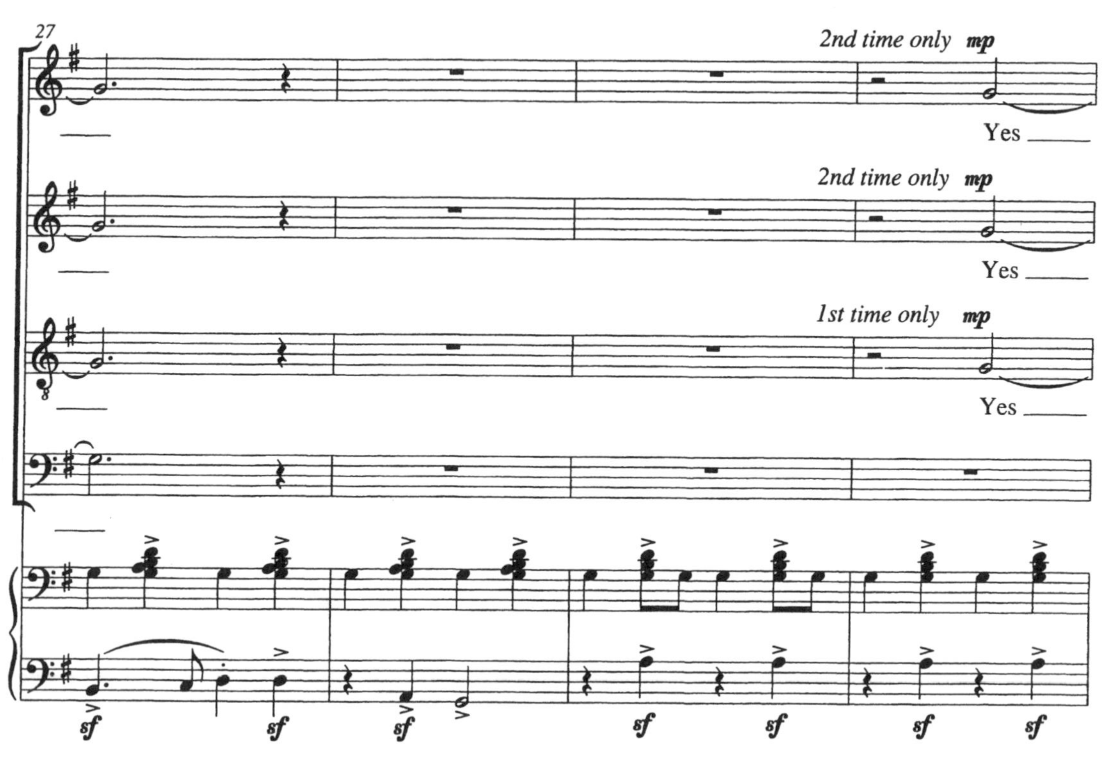

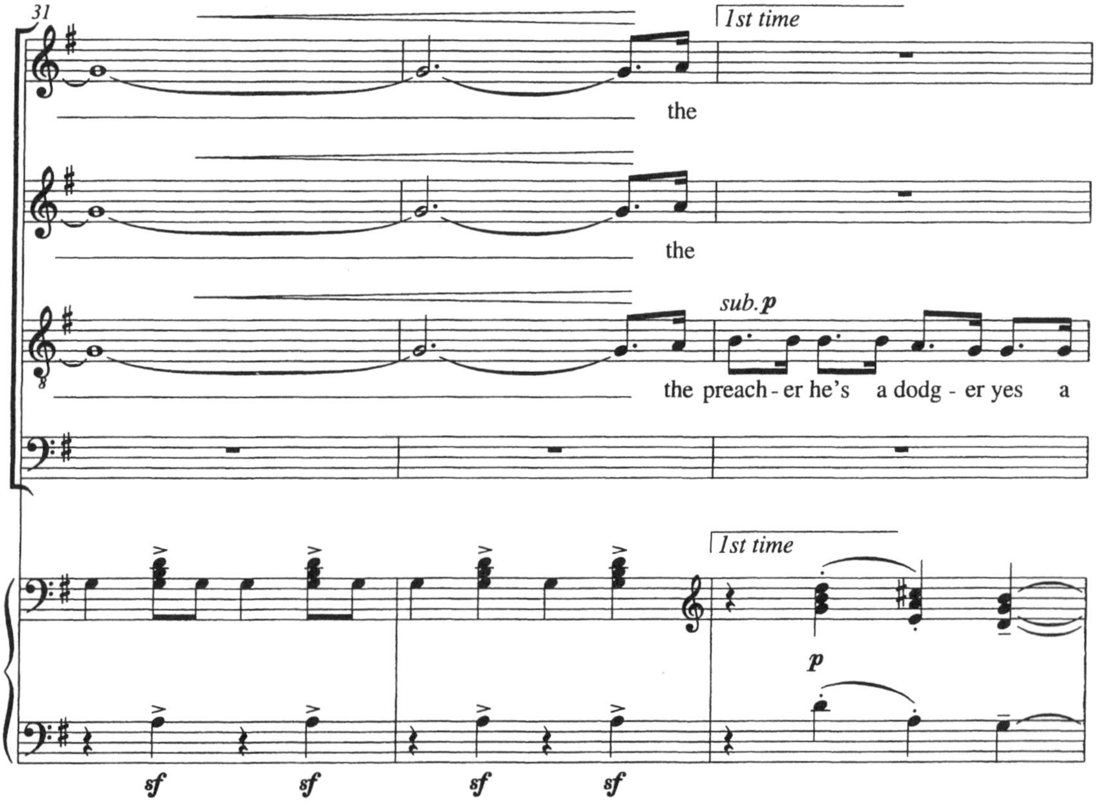
31
1st time
the
the
sub. p
the preach - er he's a dodg - er yes a
1st time
p
sf
sf
sf
sf

34
well known dodg - er, Yes the preach-er he's a dodg - er yes and I'm a dodg - er too

37
(a trifle slower)
mp
(𝄐)
a tempo
He'll preach you a gos - pel and tell you of your crimes But
(a trifle slower)
mp
p

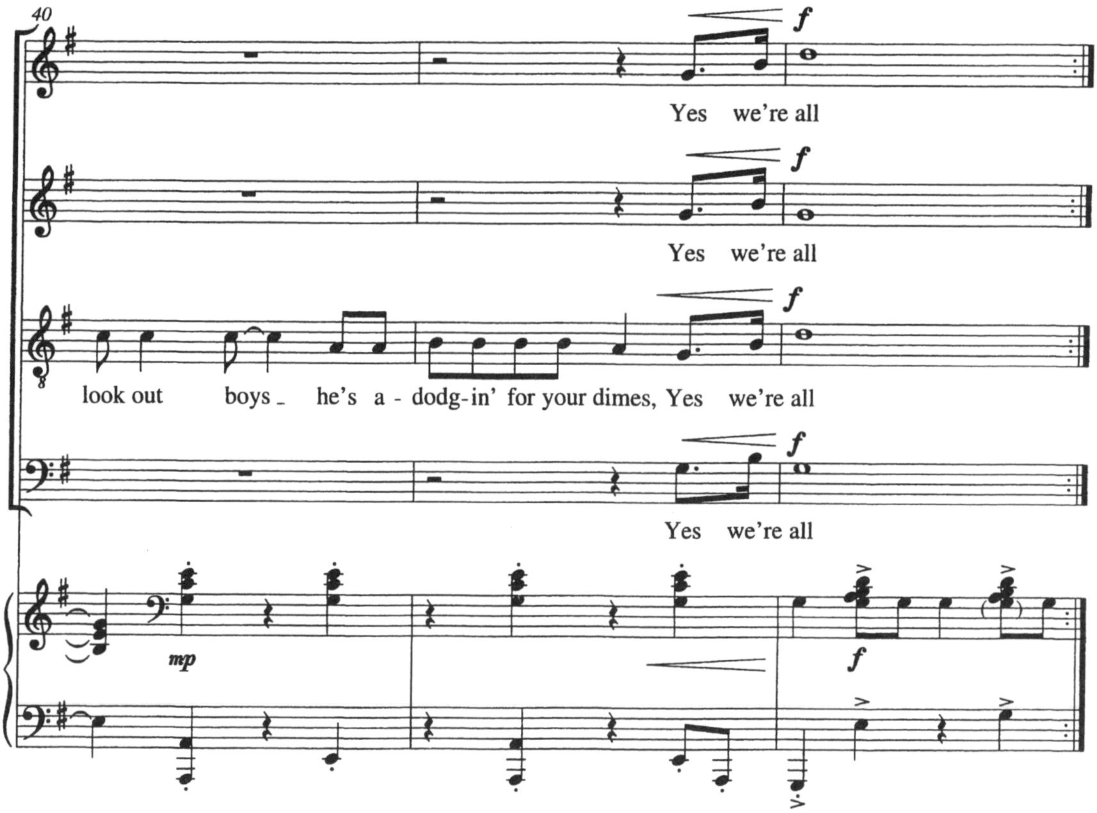

40

f

Yes we're all

f

Yes we're all

f

look out boys _ he's a - dodg-in' for your dimes, Yes we're all

f

Yes we're all

mp

f

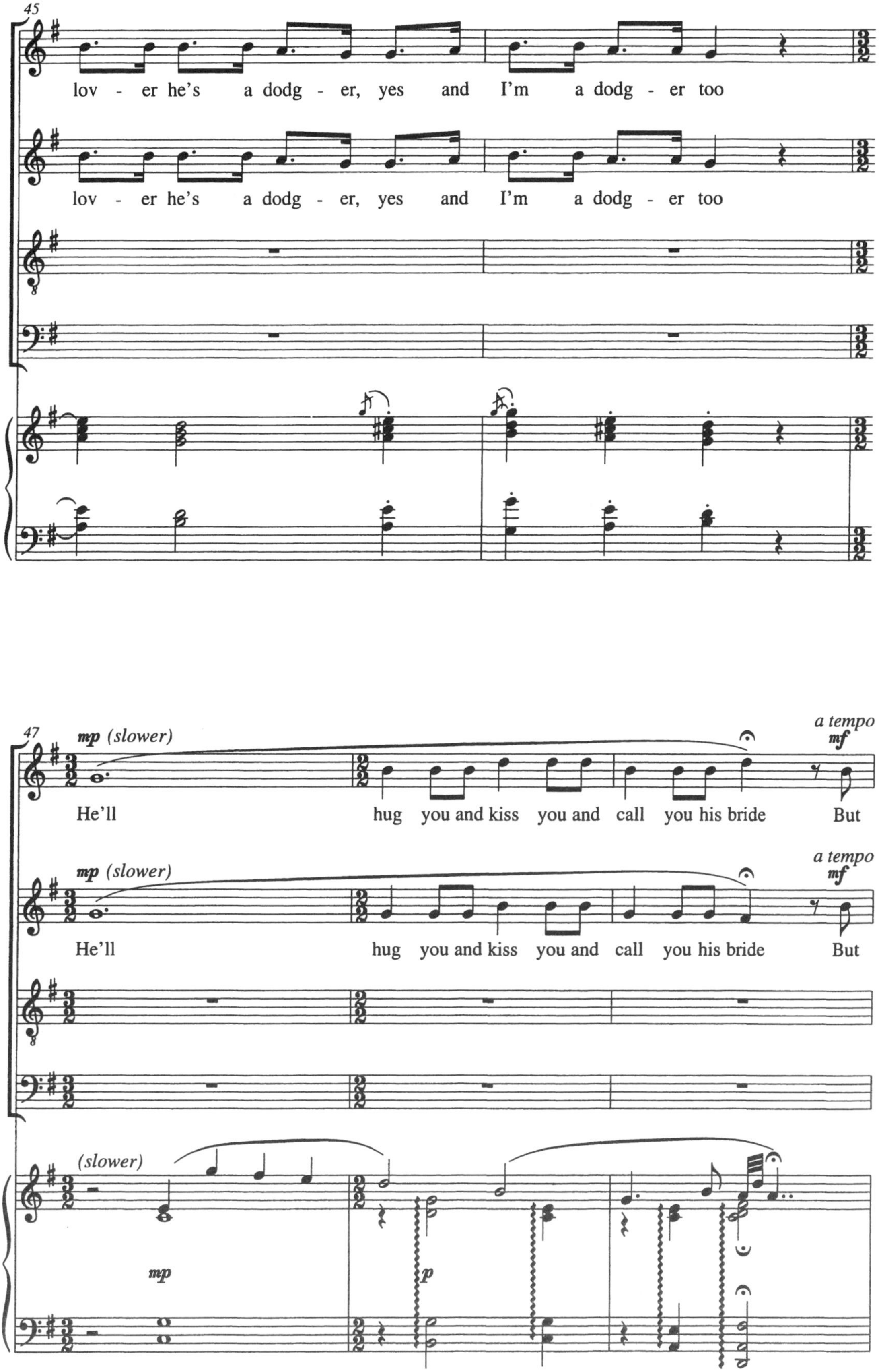

47

mp (slower) *a tempo* *mf*

He'll hug you and kiss you and call you his bride But

mp (slower) *a tempo* *mf*

He'll hug you and kiss you and call you his bride But

(slower)

mp

p

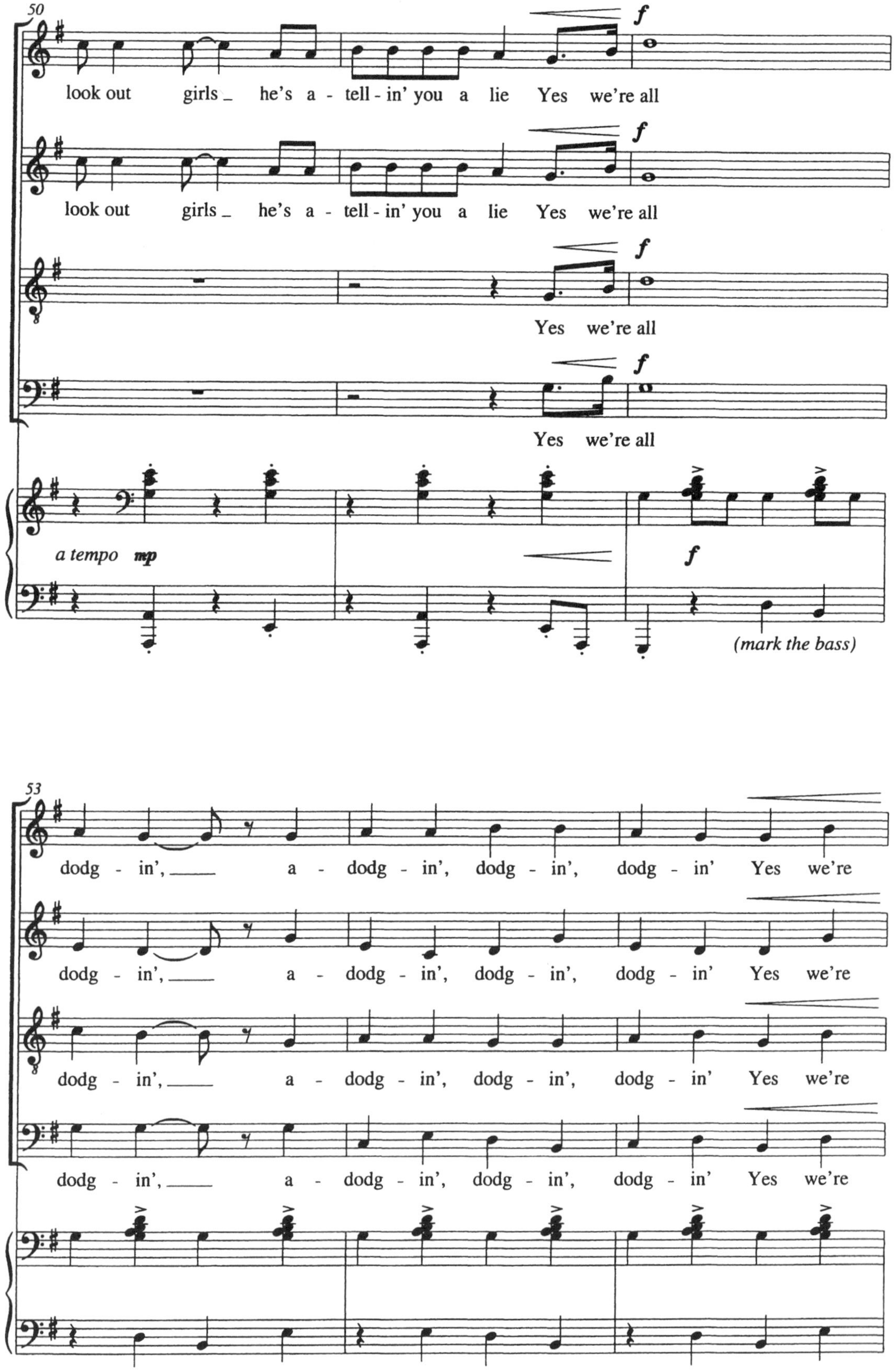

50

f

look out girls _ he's a - tell - in' you a lie Yes we're all

f

look out girls _ he's a - tell - in' you a lie Yes we're all

f

Yes we're all

f

Yes we're all

a tempo ***mp***

f

(mark the bass)

56

ff

all dodg - in' out a way through the

ff

all dodg - in' out a way through the

ff

all dodg - in' out a way through the

ff

all dodg - in' out a way through the

59

world.

world.

world.

world.

ff

sf sf sf sf sf sf sf

3. LONG TIME AGO

(Ballad)

Arranged by
AARON COPLAND
Transcribed for chorus by
IRVING FINE

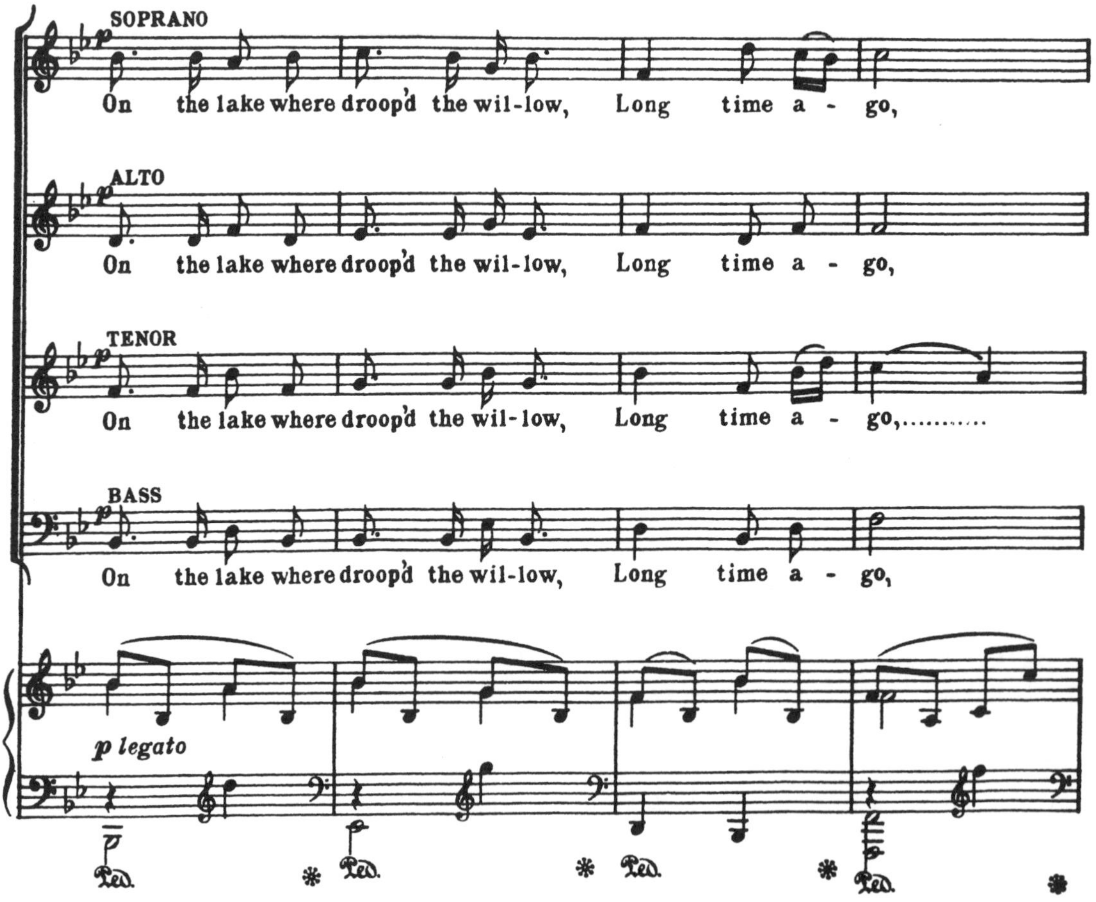

SOPRANO
p
On the lake where droop'd the wil-low, Long time a - go,

ALTO
p
On the lake where droop'd the wil-low, Long time a - go,

TENOR
p
On the lake where droop'd the wil-low, Long time a - go,..........

BASS
p
On the lake where droop'd the wil-low, Long time a - go,

p legato

mp rit. a tempo p

Where the rock threw back the bil-low, Bright - er than snow..................

mp p

Where the rock threw back the bil-low, Bright - er than snow..................

mp p

Where the rock threw back the bil-low, Bright - er than snow..................

mp p

Where the rock threw back the bil-low, Bright - er than snow..................

mp rit. a tempo mf

Ped. simile

poco
p
p
cher - ish'd high...... and low...............
But.......... with au-tumn
p
p
By high and low.
But.......... with au-tumn
p
mp
By high and low.
But with au - tumn
p
By high and low.
But with au - tumn
mf
rit.
a tempo
leaf......... she per-ish'd,
Long....... time a - go.............................
leaf........... she per-ish'd, Long time a - go.............................
leaf she per-ish'd, Long time a - go.............................
leaf she per-ish'd, Long time a - go.............................
rit.
mf a tempo

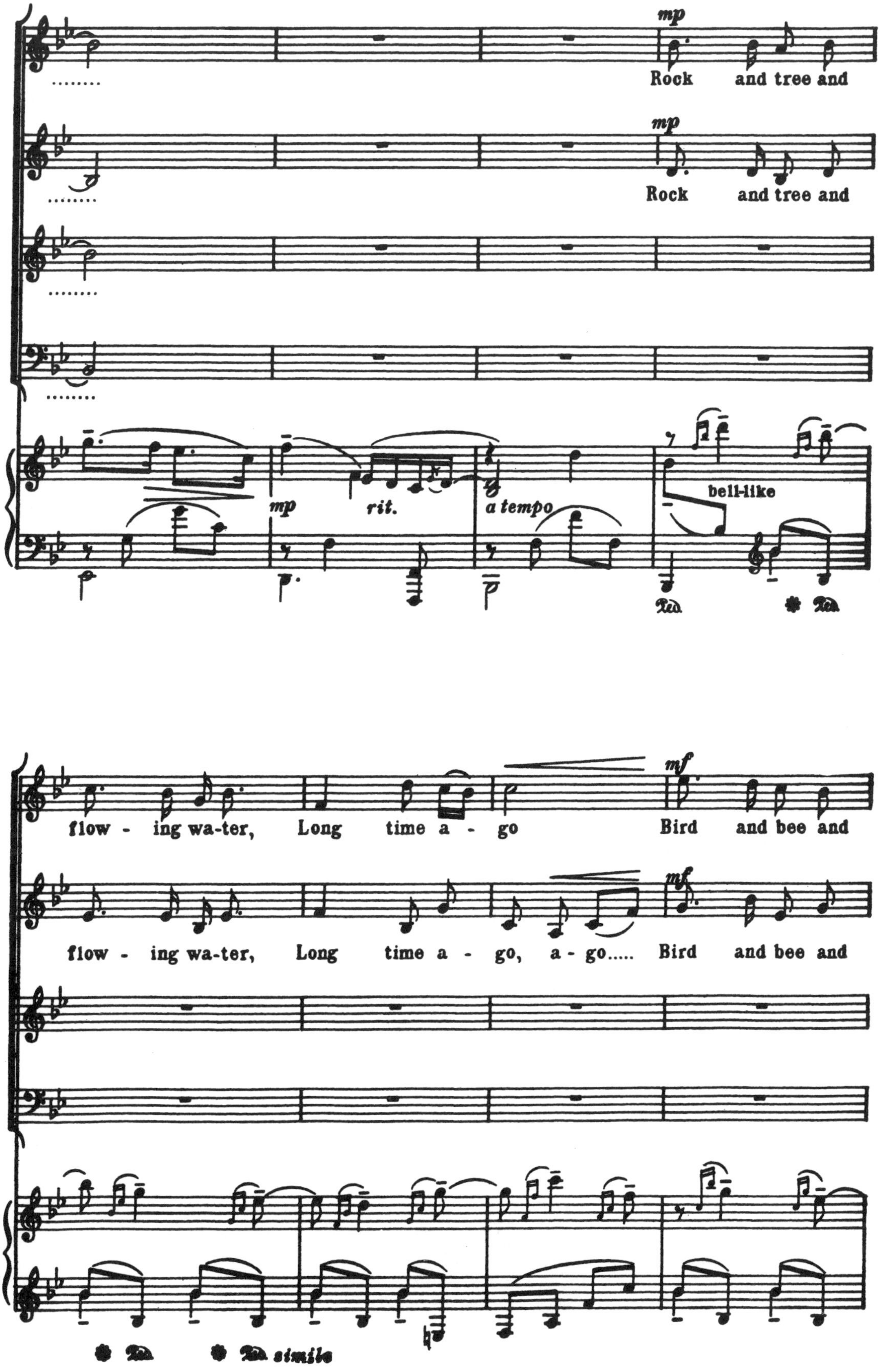
mp
Rock and tree and
mp
Rock and tree and
mp
rit.
a tempo
bell-like
Ped. * Ped.
flow - ing wa-ter, Long time a - go
mf
Bird and bee and
flow - ing wa-ter, Long time a - go, a - go.....
mf
Bird and bee and
* Ped. * Ped. simile

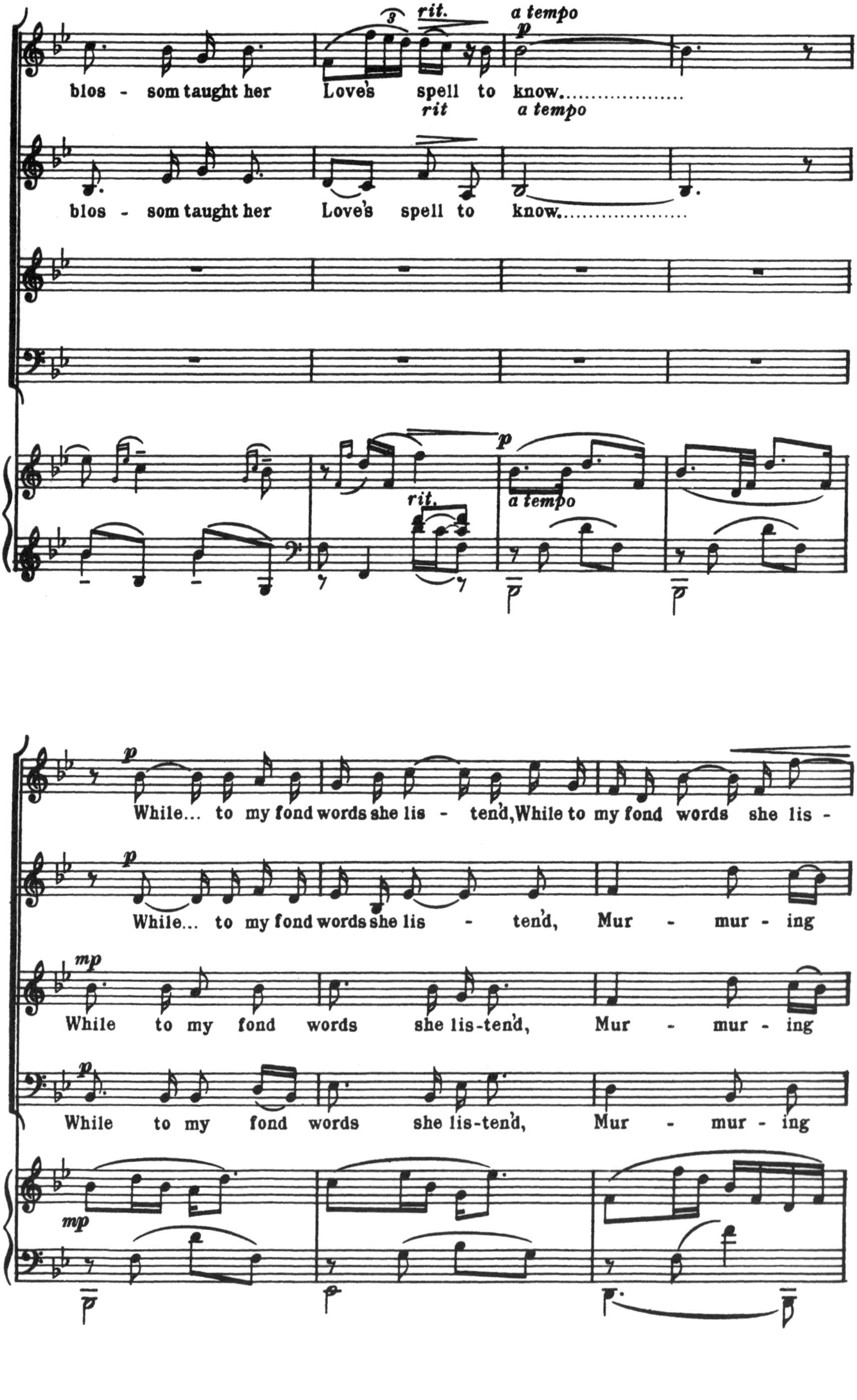

3 *rit.* *a tempo*

blos - som taught her Love's spell to know.....................

rit *a tempo*

blos - som taught her Love's spell to know.....................

rit. *a tempo*

While... to my fond words she lis - tend, While to my fond words she lis -

While... to my fond words she lis - tend, Mur - mur - ing

While to my fond words she lis-tend, Mur - mur - ing

While to my fond words she lis-tend, Mur - mur - ing

mf

- tend, Mur - m'ring low Ten - der-ly her blue eyes glis-tend

poco mf

low Ten - der-ly her blue eyes glis-tend

poco mf

low Ten - der-ly her blue eyes glis-tend

poco mf

low Ten - der-ly her blue eyes glis-tend

mf

p rit. a tempo

Long time a - go.

p

Long time a - go.

p

Long time a - go.

p

Long time a - go.

p rit. mp a tempo p pp

Ped. *

4. SIMPLE GIFTS

(Shaker Song)

Arranged by
AARON COPLAND
Transcribed for chorus by
DAVID L. BRUNNER

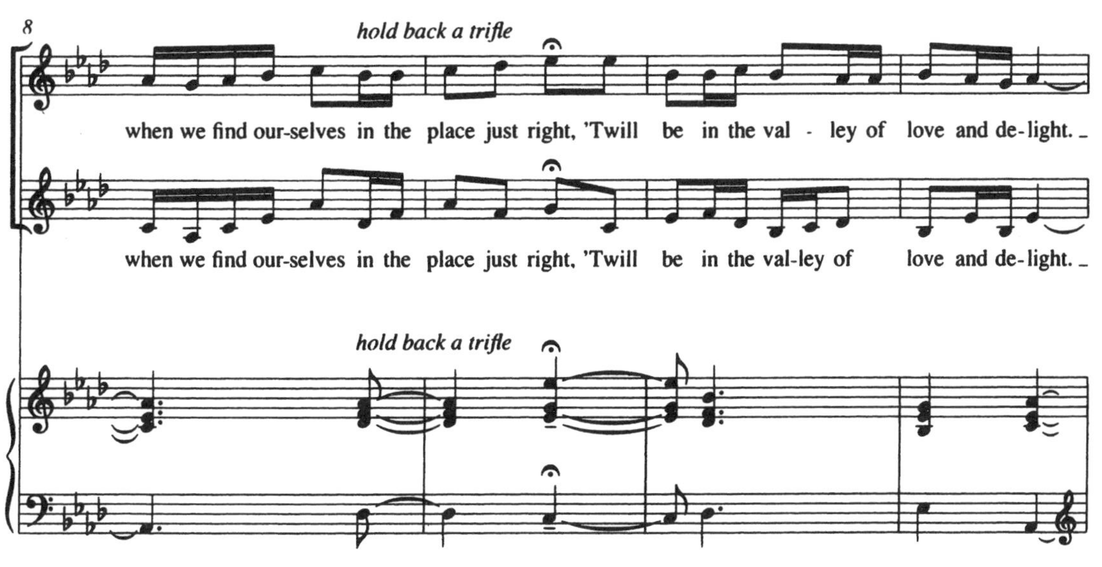

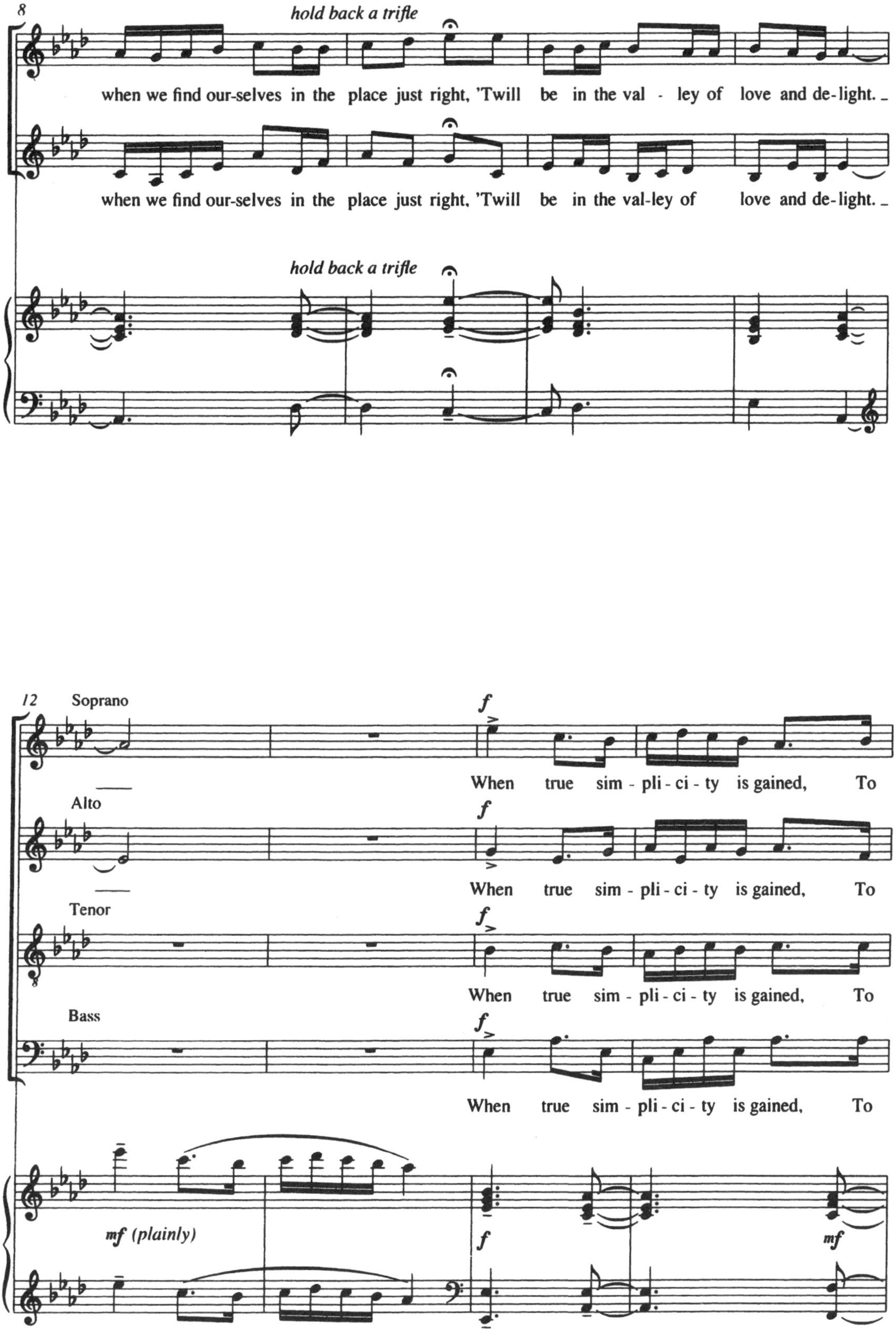

8
hold back a trifle
when we find our-selves in the place just right, 'Twill be in the val - ley of love and de-light.
when we find our-selves in the place just right, 'Twill be in the val-ley of love and de-light.
hold back a trifle
12
Soprano
f
When true sim - pli - ci - ty is gained, To
Alto
f
When true sim - pli - ci - ty is gained, To
Tenor
f
When true sim - pli - ci - ty is gained, To
Bass
f
When true sim - pli - ci - ty is gained, To
mf (plainly)
f
mf

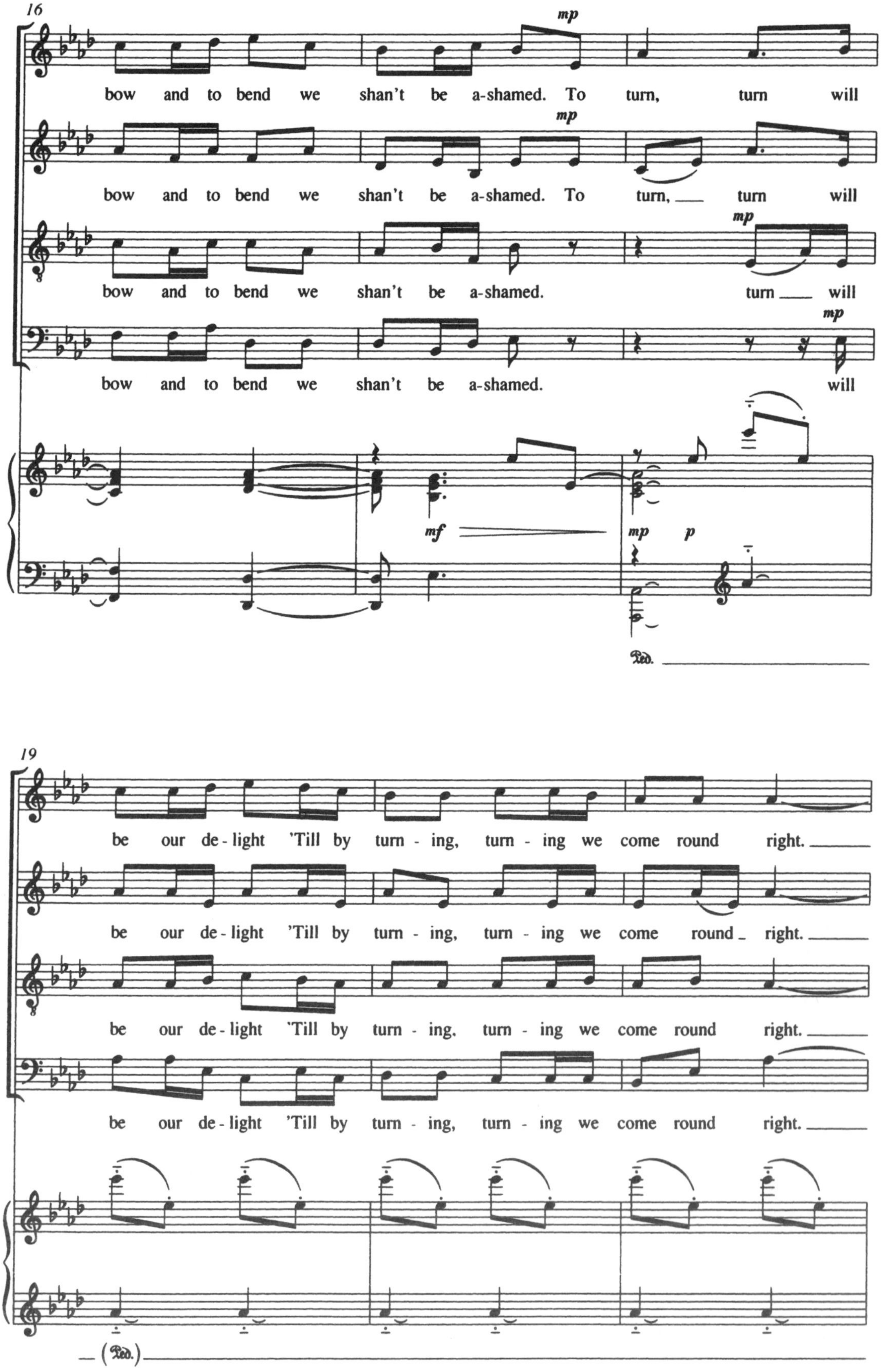
16
mp
bow and to bend we shan't be a-shamed. To turn, turn will
mp
bow and to bend we shan't be a-shamed. To turn, turn will
mp
bow and to bend we shan't be a-shamed. turn will
mp
bow and to bend we shan't be a-shamed. will
mf
mp p
Ped.
19
be our de-light 'Till by turn-ing, turn-ing we come round right.
be our de-light 'Till by turn-ing, turn-ing we come round right.
be our de-light 'Till by turn-ing, turn-ing we come round right.
be our de-light 'Till by turn-ing, turn-ing we come round right.
(Ped.)

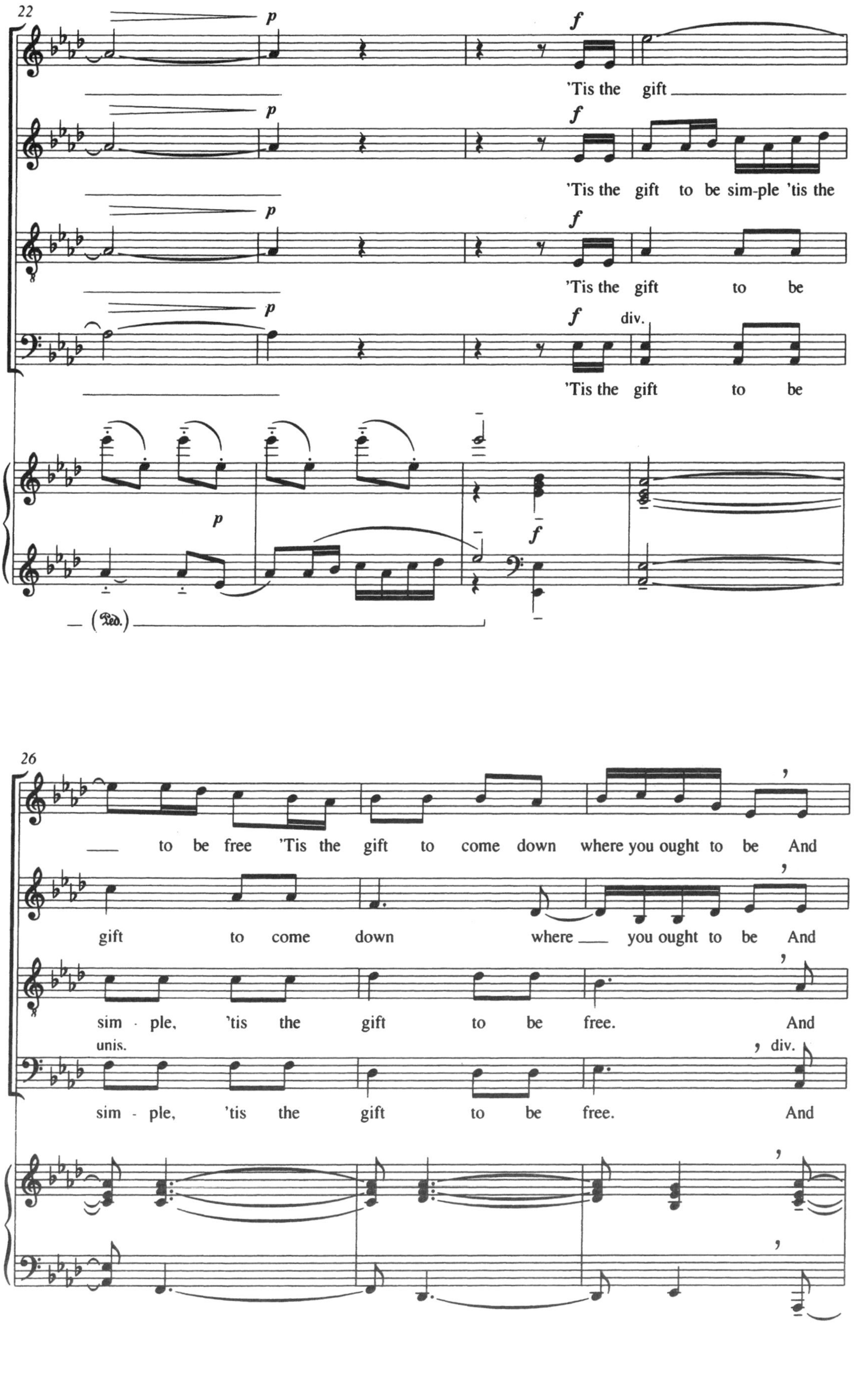

22

p f

'Tis the gift

p f

'Tis the gift to be sim-ple 'tis the

p f

'Tis the gift to be

p f div.

'Tis the gift to be

p f

(Ped.)

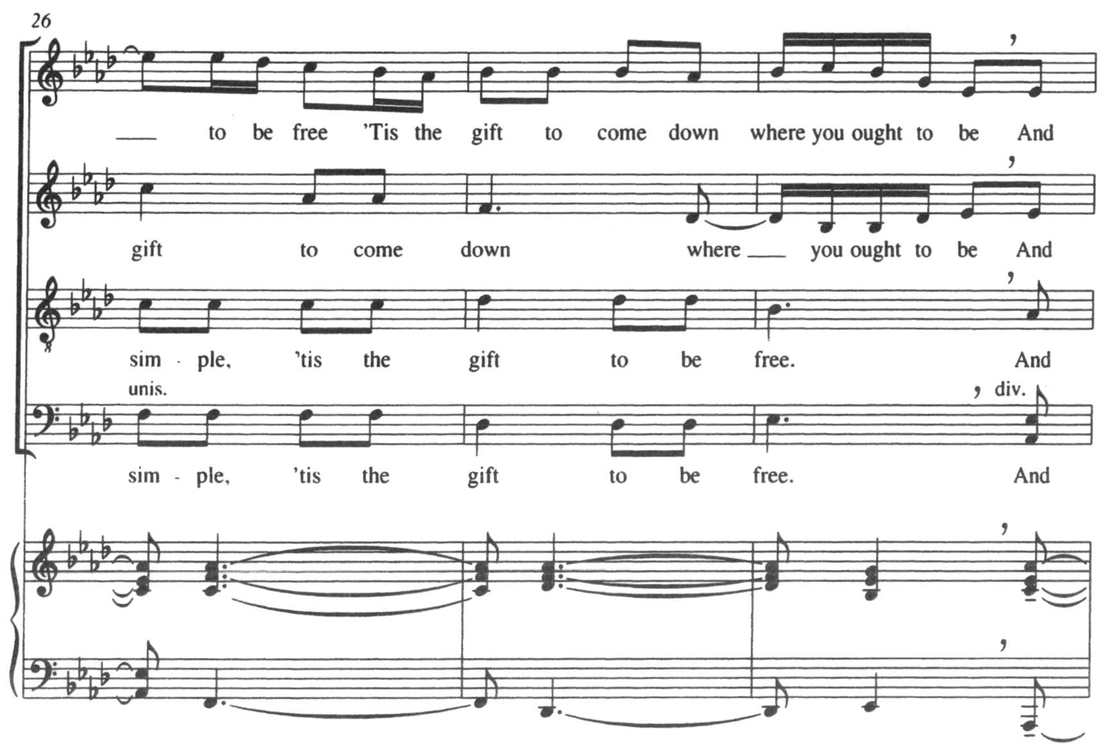

29
hold back a trifle
when in the place just right 'Twill be in the val - ley of love and de-light.
when we find our-selves in the place just right 'Twill be in the val-ley of love and de-light.
when in the place just right
unis.
when in the place just right
hold back a trifle
Ped.
33
p
rit.
p
mf
p
rit.
p
pp
(Ped.)
(dreamily)

5. I BOUGHT ME A CAT

(Children's Song)

Arranged by
AARON COPLAND
Transcribed for chorus by
IRVING FINE

For SATB (Tenor and Soprano Solos)

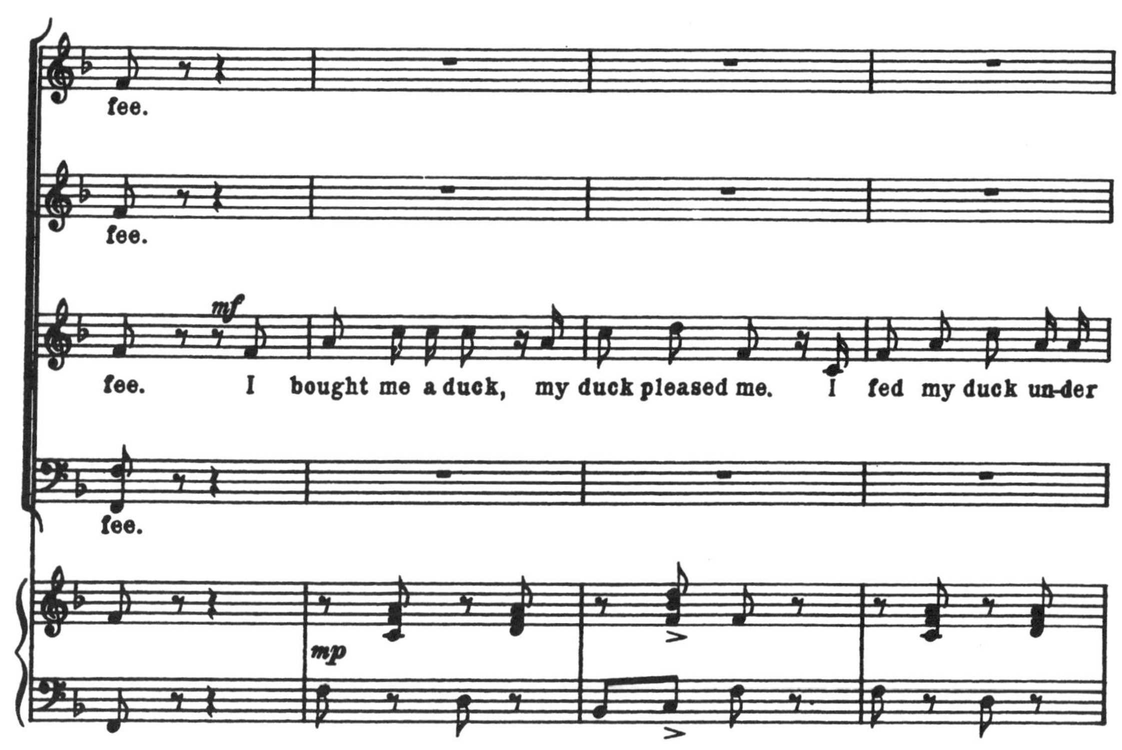
fee.
fee.
mf
fee. I bought me a duck, my duck pleased me. I fed my duck un-der
fee.
mp

p
My cat says fid-dle eye
p
My cat says fid-dle eye
SOLO
yon-der tree. My duck says "Quaa, quaa,"
TUTTI p
My cat says fid-dle eye
p
My cat says fid-dle eye
poco sf
sf
p

mf
fee. I bought me a goose, My goose pleased me I fed my goose un-der
fee.
fee.
fee.
mf

SOLO
yon-der tree My goose says "Quaw, quaw"
TUTTI p
My
p
My
mp SOLO
My duck says "Quaa, quaa"
TUTTI p
My
p
My
poco sf
(sf) (sf) (sf) (sf)

mf

cat says fid-dle eye fee. I bought me a hen, My hen pleased me

mf

cat says fid-dle eye fee. I bought me a hen, My hen pleased me I

cat says fid-dle eye fee.

mp

cat says fid-dle eye fee. My hen plea-ses me

p

mf *(mark the bass)*

I fed her un-der yon-der tree. My hen says "Shim-my shack, shim-my shack," My

fed my hen un-der yon-der tree. My hen says "Shim-my shack, shim-my shack," My

mf

My hen says "Shim-my shack, shim-my shack," My

mf

fed her un-der the tree. My

poco sf

f *(dry)*

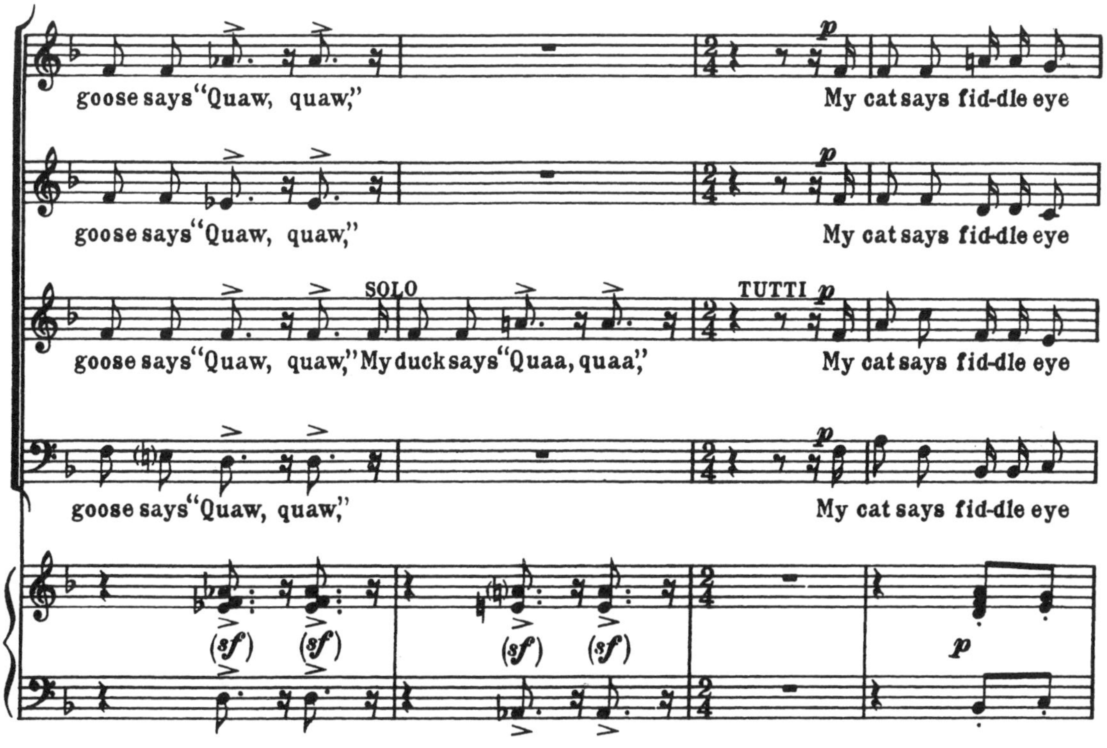

p
goose says "Quaw, quaw," My cat says fid-dle eye
p
goose says "Quaw, quaw," My cat says fid-dle eye
SOLO
TUTTI p
goose says "Quaw, quaw," My duck says "Quaa, quaa," My cat says fid-dle eye
p
goose says "Quaw, quaw," My cat says fid-dle eye
(sf) (sf) (sf) (sf)
p

mf
fee. I bought me a pig, My pig pleased me. I fed my pig un-der
mf
fee. I bought me a pig, My pig pleased me. I fed my pig un-der
mf
fee. I bought me a pig, My pig pleased me. I fed my pig un-der
mf
fee. I bought me a pig, My pig pleased me. I fed my pig un-der
f stacc., dry

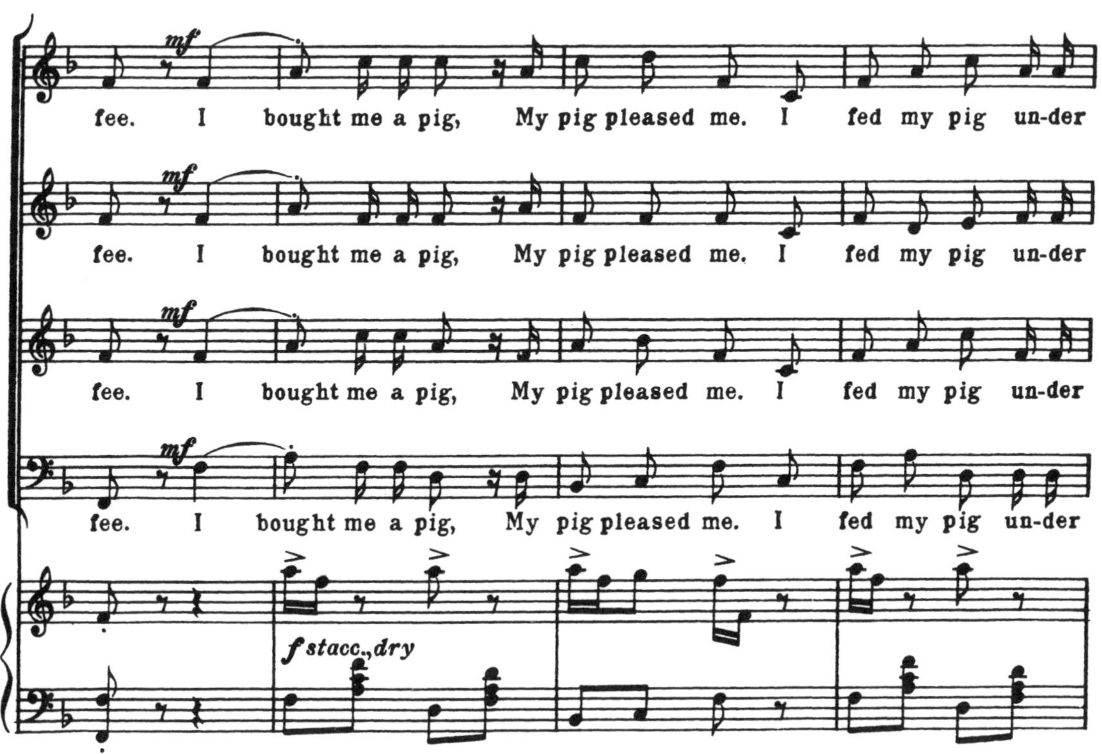

mp mf
yon - der tree. My pig says "Grif - fey, grif - fey" My

mp mf
yon - der tree. My pig says "Grif - fey, grif - fey" My

mf
yon - der tree. My

yon - der tree.

mf
f (dry)
(sf) (sf)

SOLO
hen says Shim-my shack, shim-my shack" My goose says "Quaw, quaw" My

hen says Shim-my shack, shim-my shack" My goose says "Quaw, quaw"

hen says Shim-my shack, shim-my shack" My goose says "Quaw, quaw"

mf
My goose says "Quaw, quaw"

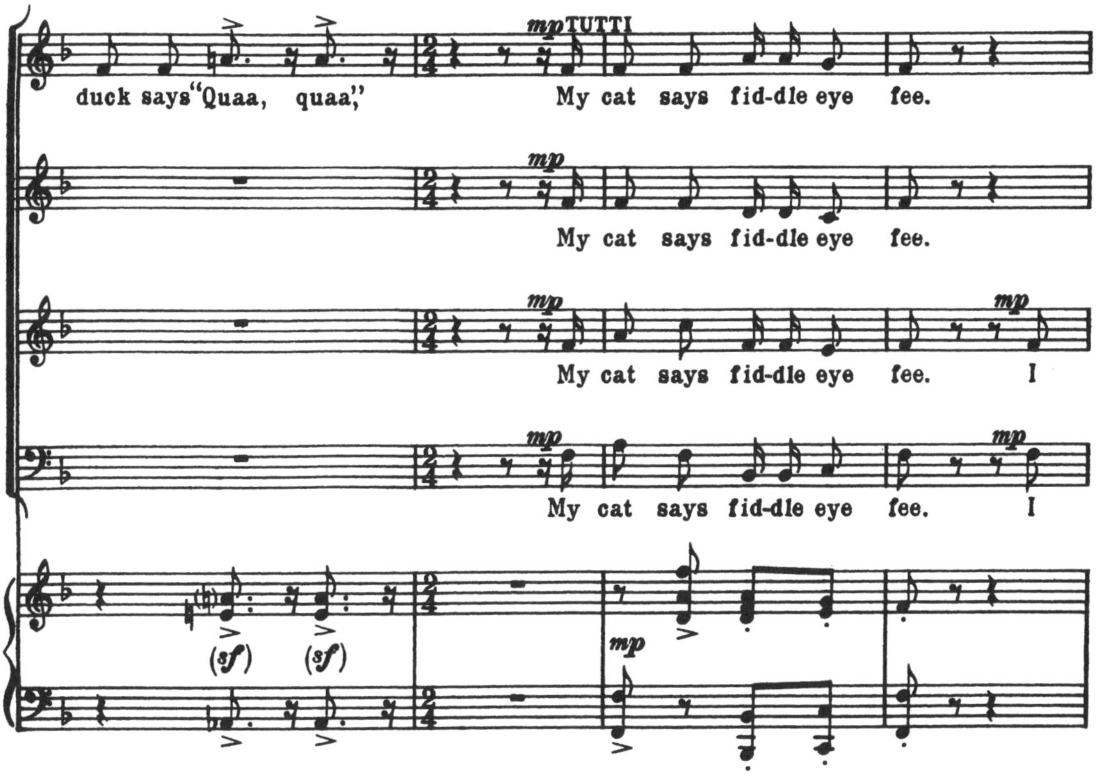

duck says "Quaa, quaa," *mp* TUTTI My cat says fid-dle eye fee.

mp My cat says fid-dle eye fee.

mp My cat says fid-dle eye fee. *mp* I

mp My cat says fid-dle eye fee. *mp* I

(*sf*) (*sf*) *mp*

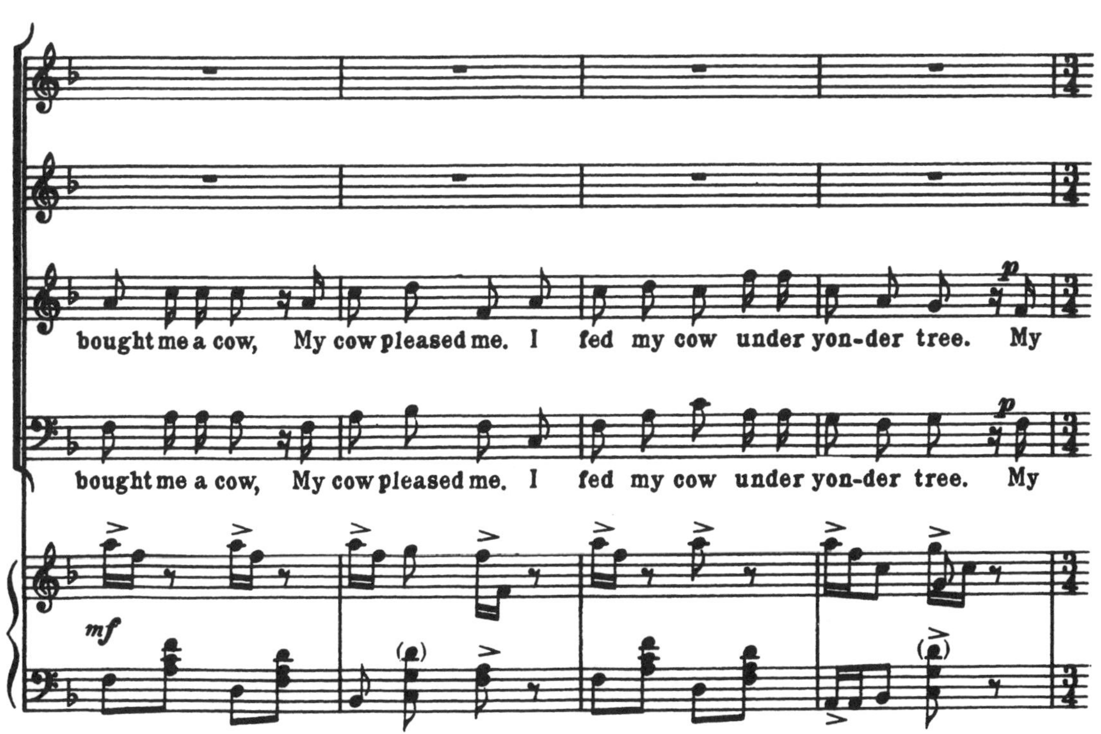

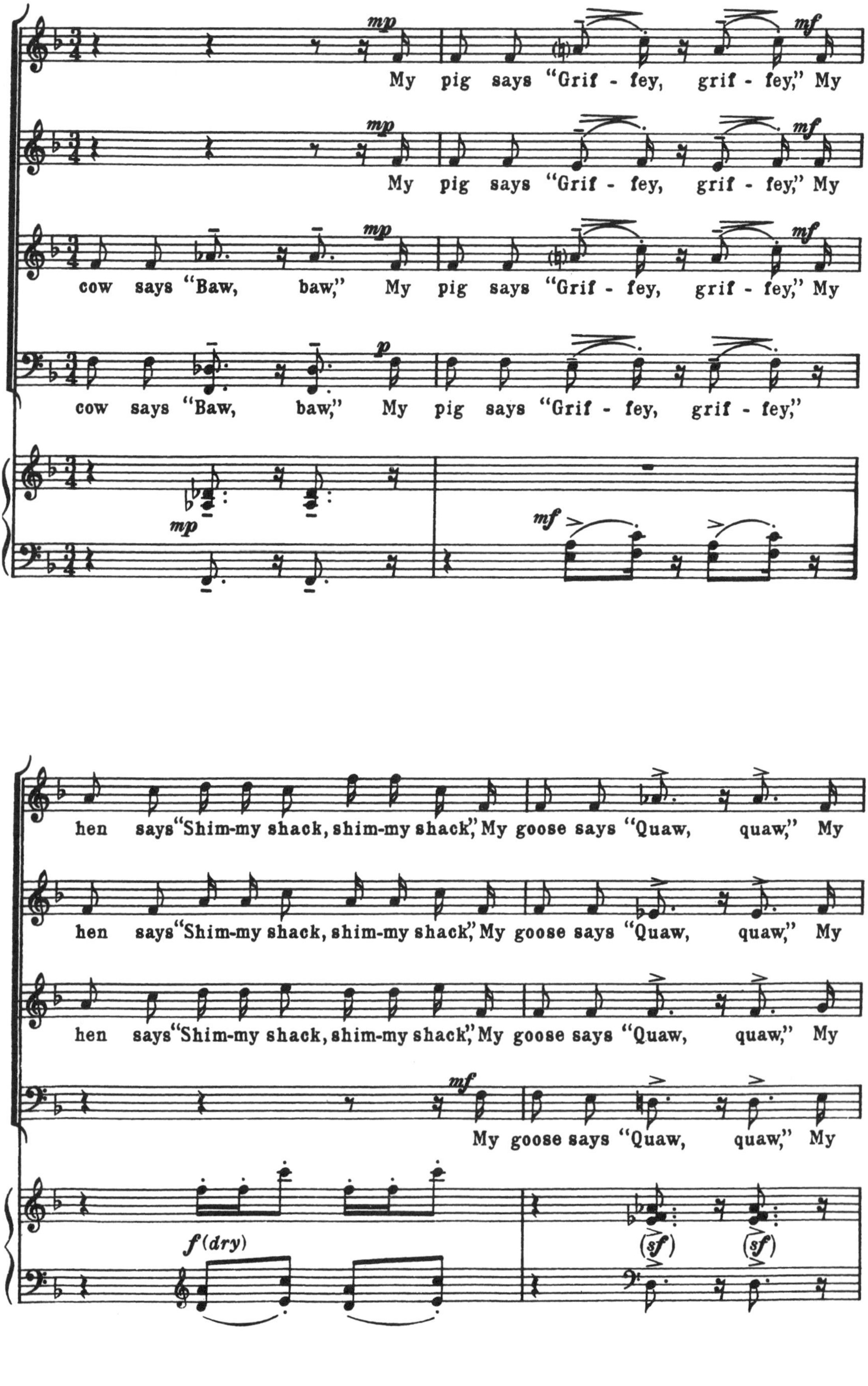

mp mf
My pig says "Grif - fey, grif - fey," My

mp mf
My pig says "Grif - fey, grif - fey," My

mp mf
cow says "Baw, baw," My pig says "Grif - fey, grif - fey," My

p
cow says "Baw, baw," My pig says "Grif - fey, grif - fey,"

mp mf

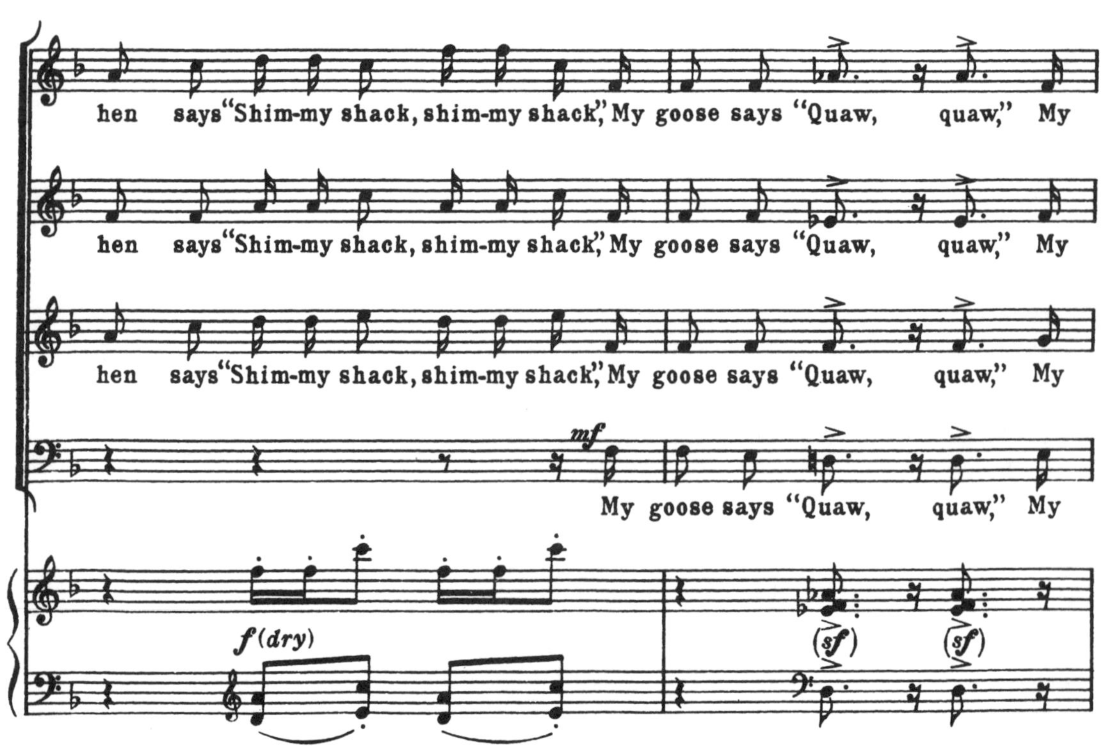

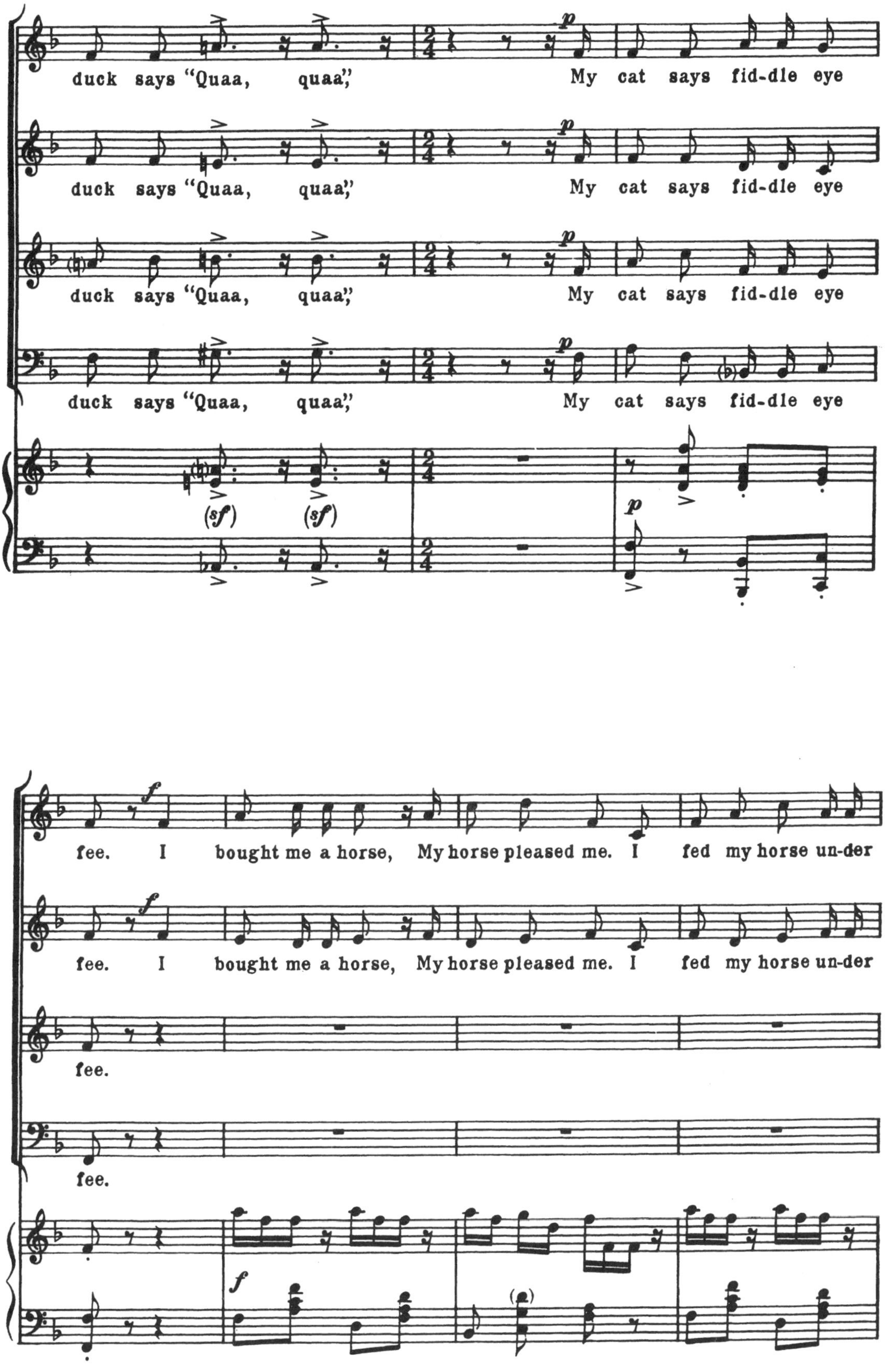

duck says "Quaa, quaa," My cat says fid-dle eye
duck says "Quaa, quaa," My cat says fid-dle eye
duck says "Quaa, quaa," My cat says fid-dle eye
duck says "Quaa, quaa," My cat says fid-dle eye
fee. I bought me a horse, My horse pleased me. I fed my horse un-der
fee. I bought me a horse, My horse pleased me. I fed my horse un-der
fee.
fee.

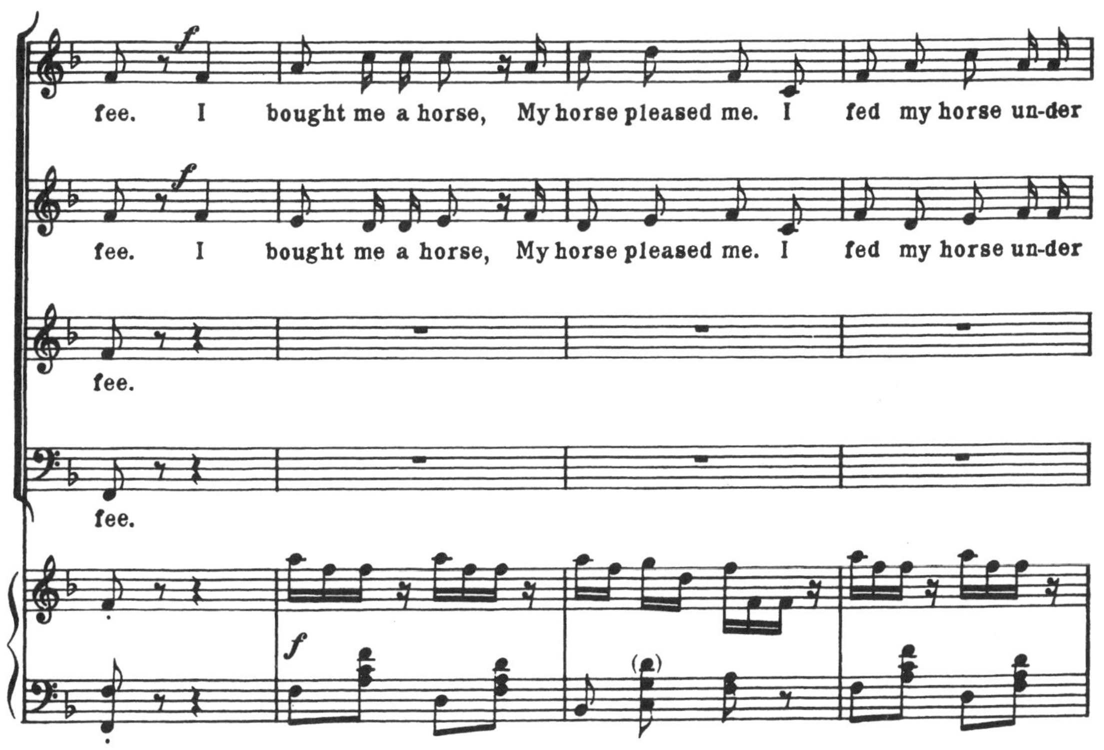

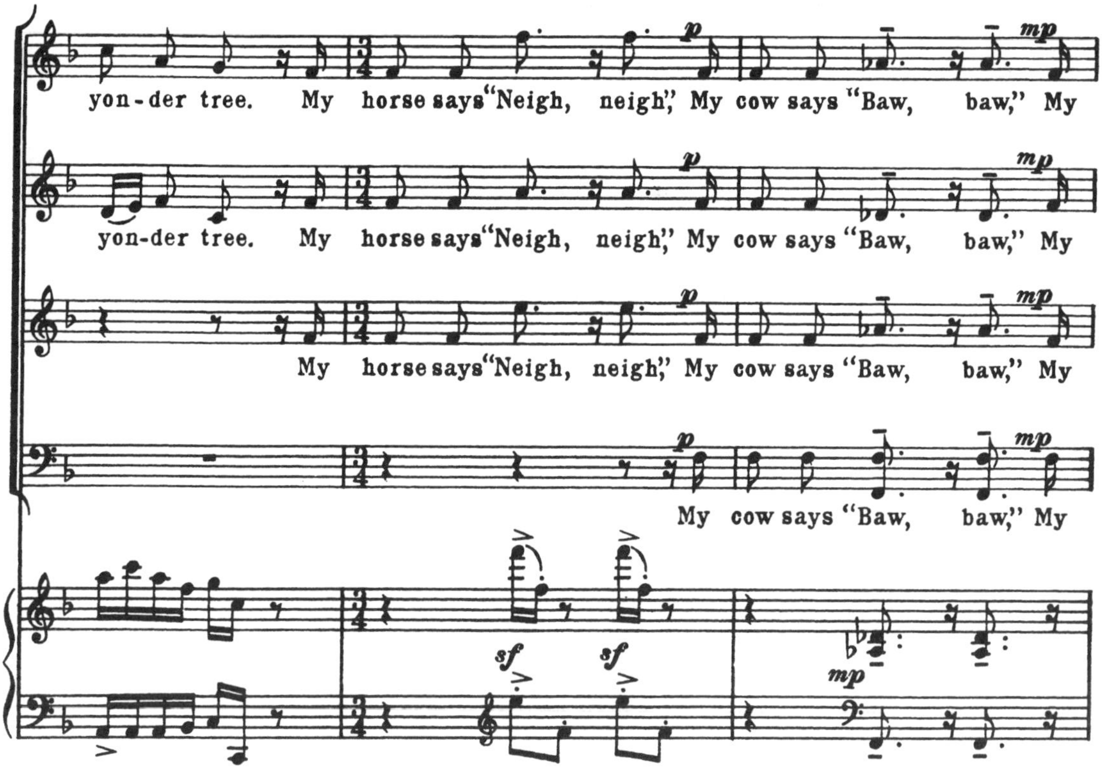
yon-der tree. My horse says "Neigh, neigh," My cow says "Baw, baw," My
yon-der tree. My horse says "Neigh, neigh," My cow says "Baw, baw," My
My horse says "Neigh, neigh," My cow says "Baw, baw," My
My cow says "Baw, baw," My

pig says "Grif - fey, grif - fey," My hen says Shim-my shack, shim-my shack," My
pig says "Grif - fey, grif - fey," My hen says Shim-my shack, shim-my shack," My
pig says "Grif - fey, grif - fey," My hen says Shim-my shack, shim-my shack," My
pig says "Grif - fey, grif - fey, My
f (dry)

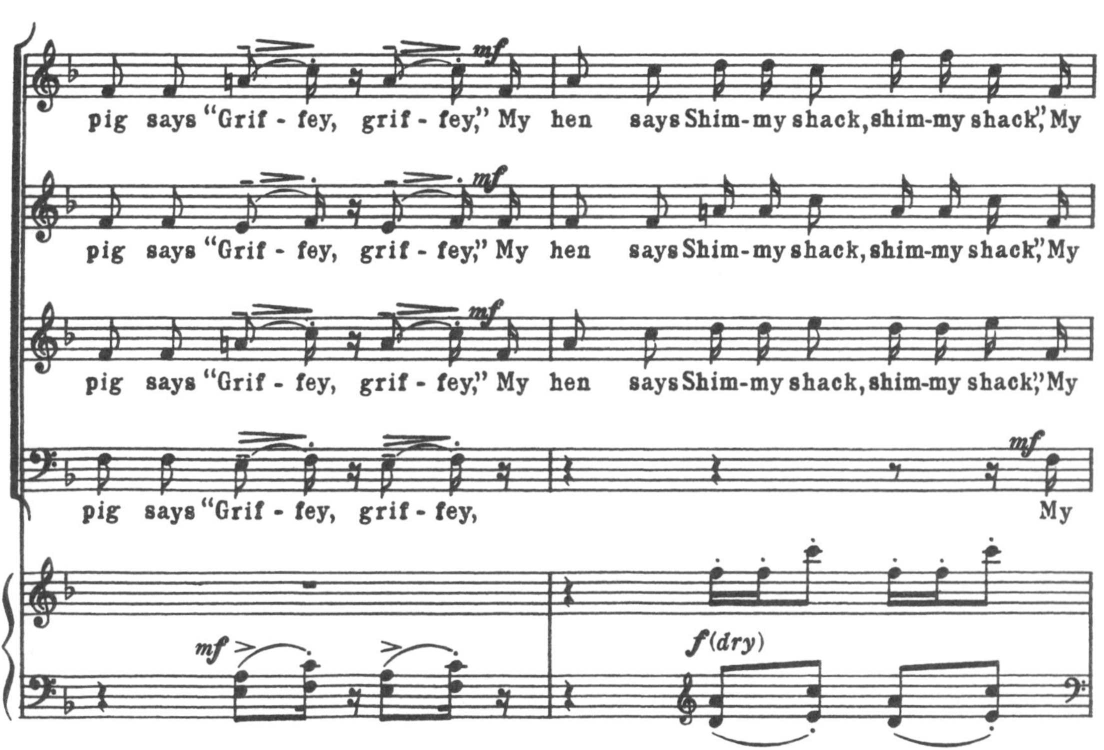

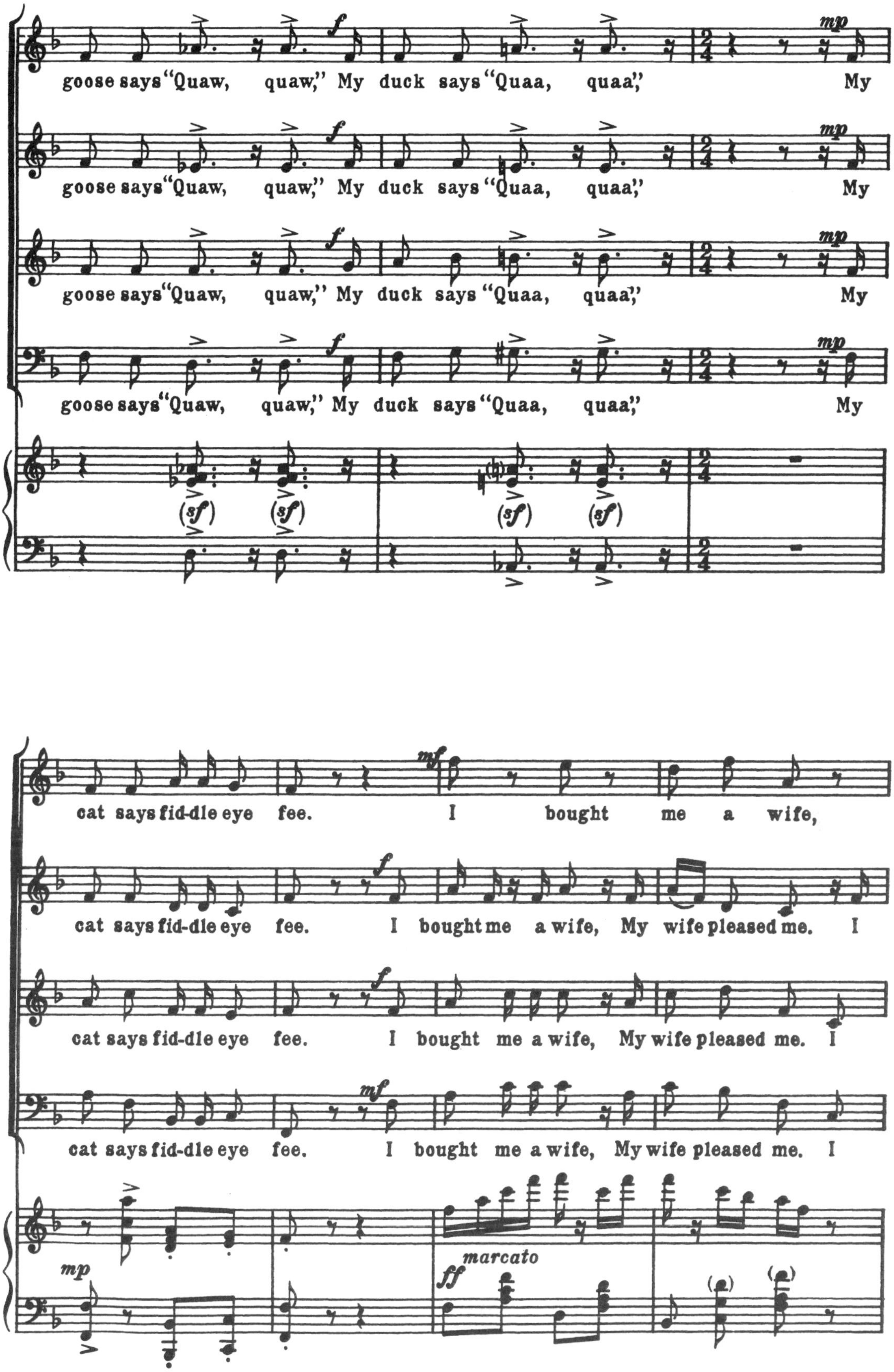

cat says fid-dle eye fee. I bought me a wife,

cat says fid-dle eye fee. I bought me a wife, My wife pleased me. I

cat says fid-dle eye fee. I bought me a wife, My wife pleased me. I

cat says fid-dle eye fee. I bought me a wife, My wife pleased me. I

marcato

mp
f
fed her under the tree. My wife says "Hon-ey, hon-ey" My
fed my wife un-der yon - der tree. My wife says "Hon-ey, hon-ey" My
fed my wife un-der yon - der tree. My wife says "Hon-ey, hon-ey" My
fed my wife un-der yon - der tree. My wife says "Hon-ey, hon-ey" My
mf
sf
horse says "Neigh, neigh" My cow says "Baw, baw" My pig says "Griffey, grif-fey" My
horse says "Neigh, neigh" My cow says "Baw, baw" My pig says "Griffey, grif-fey" My
horse says "Neigh, neigh" My cow says "Baw, baw" My pig says "Griffey, grif-fey" My
horse says "Neigh, neigh" My cow says "Baw, baw" My pig says "Griffey, grif-fey"

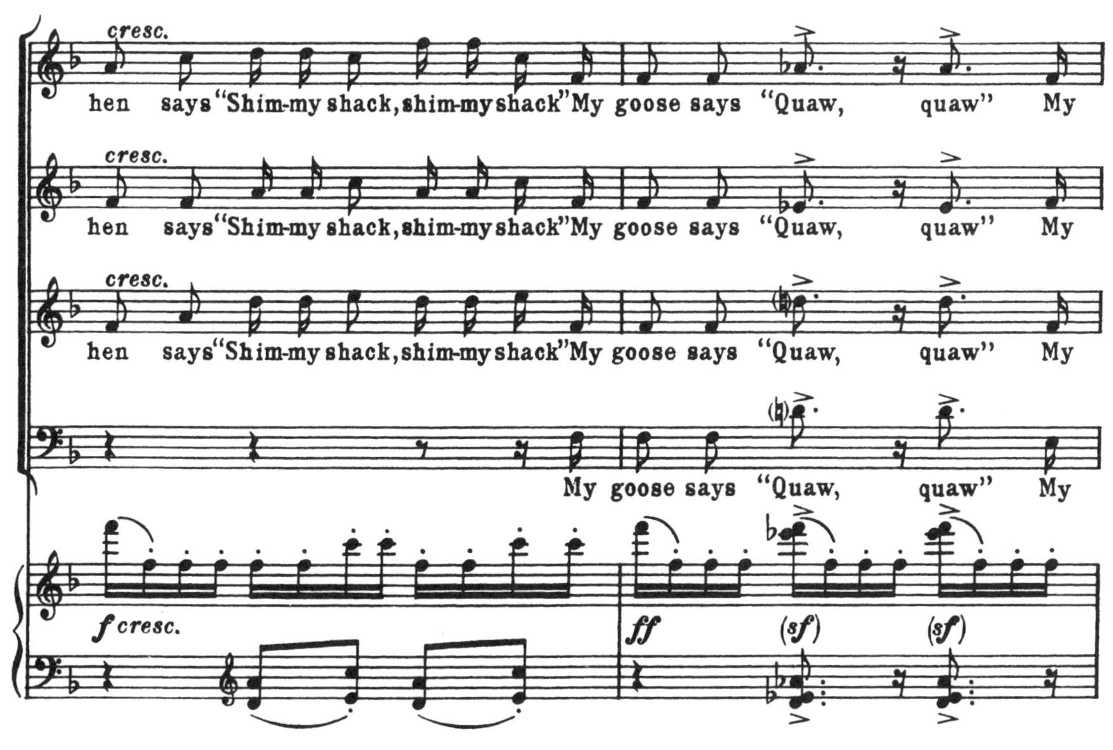
cresc.
hen says "Shim-my shack, shim-my shack" My goose says "Quaw, quaw" My
cresc.
hen says "Shim-my shack, shim-my shack" My goose says "Quaw, quaw" My
cresc.
hen says "Shim-my shack, shim-my shack" My goose says "Quaw, quaw" My
My goose says "Quaw, quaw" My
f cresc.
ff
(sf)
(sf)

duck says "Quaa, quaa"
ff
My cat says fid-dle eye fee.
duck says "Quaa, quaa"
ff
My cat says fid-dle eye fee.
duck says "Quaa, quaa"
ff
My cat says fid-dle eye fee.
duck says "Quaa, quaa"
ff
My cat says fid-dle eye fee.
(sf)
(sf)
fff
sf

Second Set

1. THE LITTLE HORSES

(Lullaby)

Arranged by
AARON COPLAND
Transcribed for chorus by
DAVID L. BRUNNER

Faster and rhythmically precise (starting a little slowly)
mp
Blacks and bays, Dap-ples and grays, Coach and six-a lit-tle hor - ses.
mp
Blacks and bays, Dap-ples and grays, Coach and six - a lit-tle hor - ses.
mp
Blacks and grays, Dap-ples and grays, six-a lit-tle
mp
Blacks and bays, Dap-ples and six - a lit-tle hor - ses.
Faster and rhythmically precise (starting a little slowly)
p (a little dry)
Tempo II (♩= 76)
mf (with a slight accent)
f hold back
Blacks and grays and Dap-ples and grays, and dap-ples and grays,... and
mf
f
Blacks and bays, dap-ples and grays, Coach
mf
f
hor - ses. Dap-ples and Coach
mf
f
Blacks and bays and Coach
Tempo II (♩= 76)
mp
cresc.
f hold back

19

As at first *(slowly)* *(in the background)*

pp

six - a lit - tle hor - ses. Oh

(in the background) *pp*

Oh

p

Hush you bye,

p

Hush you bye,

As at first *(slowly)*

mf *mf* *p*

24

Oh Hush you bye, Hush

Oh Hush you bye, Hush

Don't you cry, Go to sleep - y lit - tle ba - by. When you wake, You'll

Don't you cry, Go to sleep - y lit - tle ba - by. When you wake, You'll

(softly)

Ped.

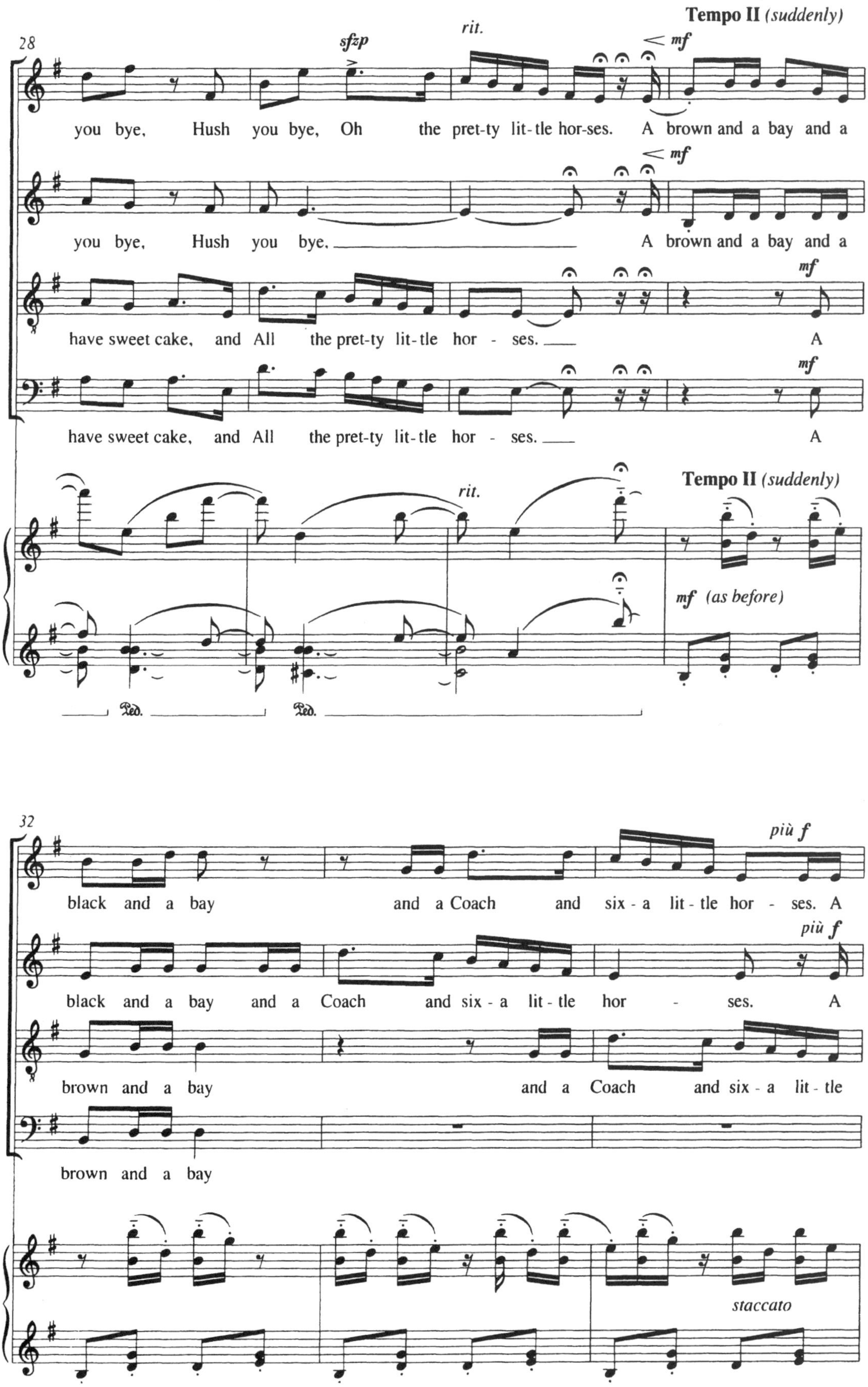
Tempo II (suddenly)
28
sfzp
rit.
mf
you bye, Hush you bye, Oh the pret-ty lit-tle hor-ses. A brown and a bay and a
mf
you bye, Hush you bye, A brown and a bay and a
mf
have sweet cake, and All the pret-ty lit-tle hor - ses. A
mf
have sweet cake, and All the pret-ty lit-tle hor - ses. A
rit.
Tempo II (suddenly)
mf (as before)
Ped.
Ped.
32
più f
black and a bay and a Coach and six - a lit - tle hor - ses. A
più f
black and a bay and a Coach and six - a lit - tle hor - ses. A
brown and a bay and a Coach and six - a lit - tle
brown and a bay
staccato

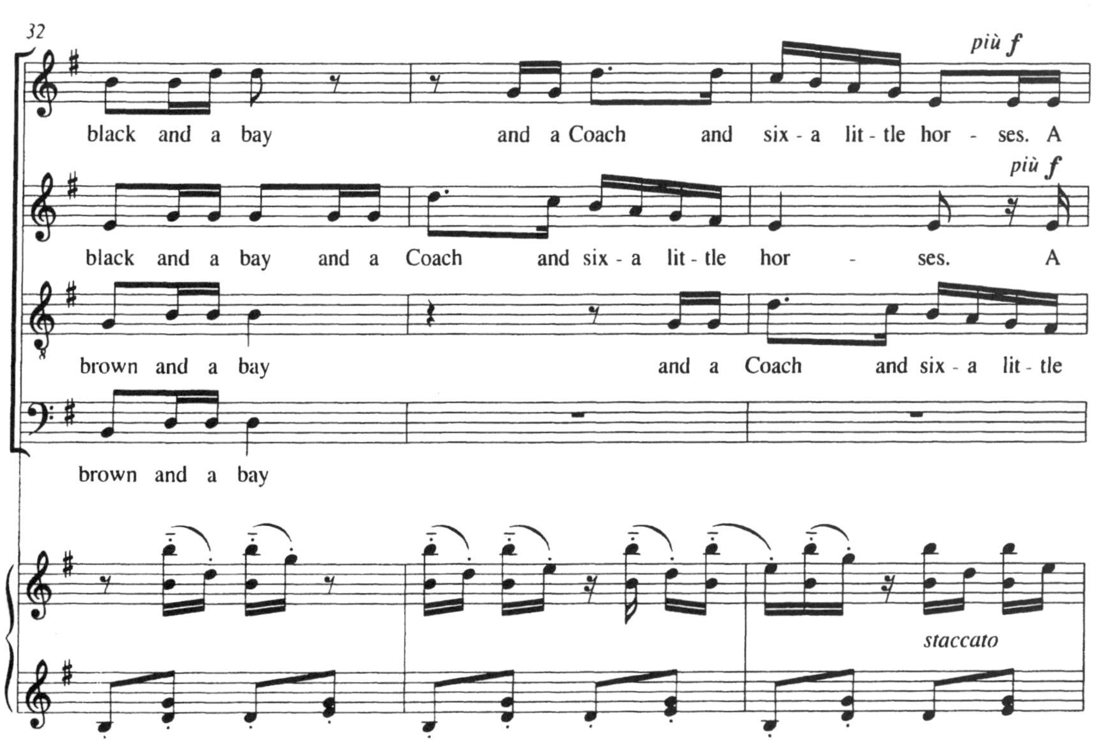

35
black and a bay and a brown and a gray and a Coach
black and a bay and a brown and a gray and a Coach
più f
hor - ses. A black and a bay and a brown and a gray and a Coach
A black and a bay and a brown and a gray and a Coach
(no ritard.)
più f
cresc.
39
long
mp
ad lib.
As at first (slowly)
and six - a lit - tle hor - ses.
and six - a lit - tle hor - ses.
As at first (slowly)
f
a tempo
mf

44
pp legato (almost sotto voce)
Hush you bye, Don't you cry. Oh you pret-ty lit-tle ba
pp legato (almost sotto voce)
mp
Hush you bye, Don't you cry, Oh you pret-ty lit-tle ba - by. Go to sleep-y lit-tle
pp legato (almost sotto voce)
Hush you bye, Don't you cry, Hush you bye, Hush you
pp legato (almost sotto voce)
Hush you bye, Don't you cry, Hush you bye, Hush you
p
mp
49
p poco
ad lib.
by Oh you pret-ty lit-tle ba - by.
p poco
ad lib.
ba by. Oh you pret-ty lit-tle ba - by.
p poco
bye. Oh
p poco
bye. Oh
p
mp

2. ZION'S WALLS

(Revivalist Song)

Arranged by
AARON COPLAND
Transcribed for chorus by
GLENN KOPONEN

7
fa - thers and moth - ers, Come sis - ters and broth - ers, Come
f
Come sis - ters and broth - ers, Come
f
Come
f
Come
Ped. * Ped. * Ped. * Ped. *
9
join us in sing - ing the prais - es of Zi - on.
join us in sing- ing the prais - es of Zi - on.
join us in sing - ing the prais - es of Zi - on, the prais - es of
join us in sing-ing the prais - es of Zi - on, the prais- es of
Ped. * Ped. * Ped. * Ped. *

11

O fa - thers don't_ you

O fa - thers don't_ you

Zi - on. O fa - thers don't you

Zi - on. O fa - thers don't you

f

11

f

senza Ped.

Ped. * Ped. * Ped.

14

, p sub.

feel de-ter-mined to meet_ with-in_ the walls_ of Zi - on. We'll

feel de-ter-mined to meet_ with-in_ the walls_ of Zi - on. We'll

feel de-ter-mined to meet with-in the walls of Zi - on. We'll

feel de-ter-mined to meet with-in the walls of Zi - on. We'll

14

p sub.

Ped. *

17
(no break)
crescendo
shout and go round, shout and go round, shout and go round,
shout and go round, we'll shout and go round, we'll shout and go round, we'll
div.
shout, we'll shout, we'll shout, we'll
shout, we'll shout, we'll shout, we'll
Ped.
20
molto
f
shout and go round, shout, the walls of Zi-on, Zi -
shout and go round the walls of Zi-on, the walls of Zi-on.
unis.
shout, we'll shout, the walls of Zi-on.
shout, we'll shout the walls of Zi-on, the walls of Zi -

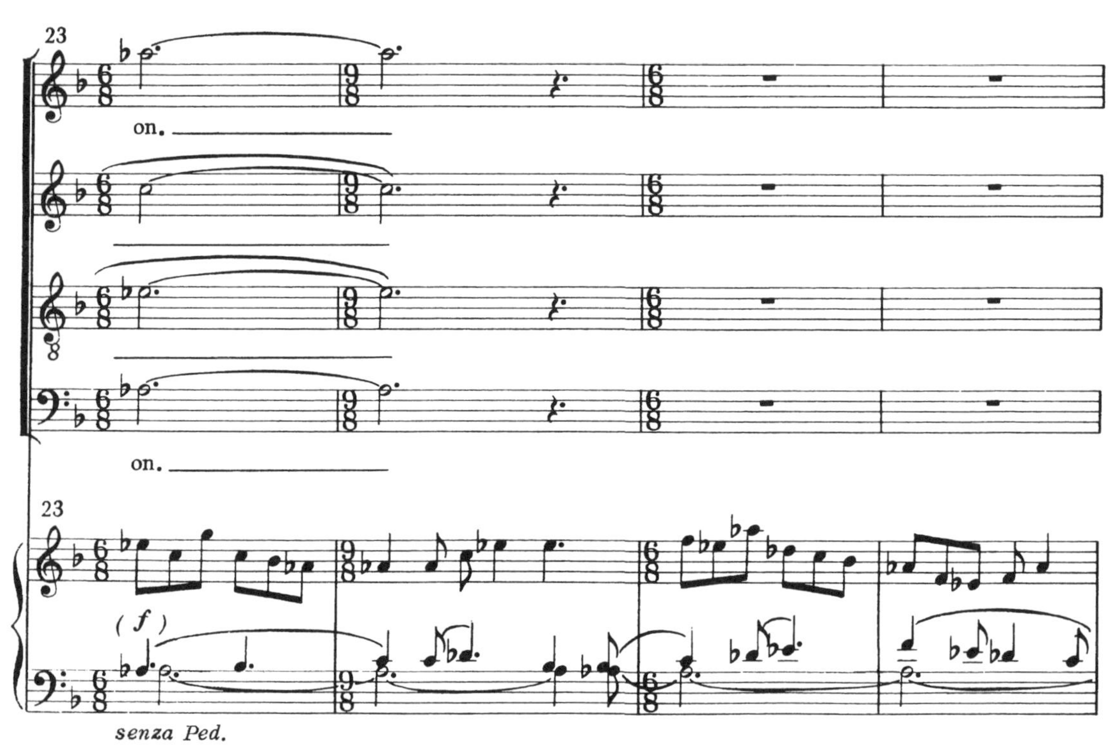

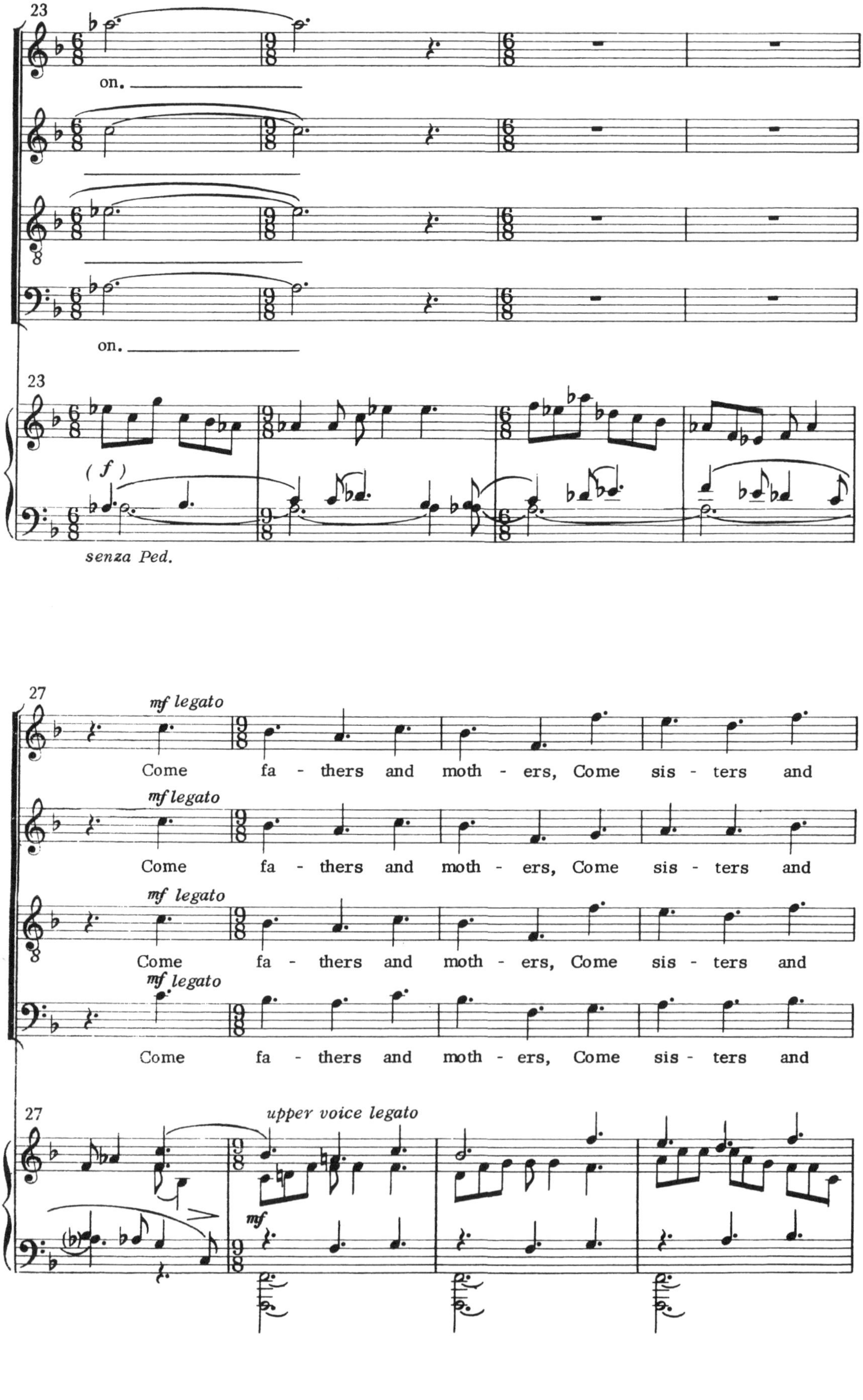

27

mf legato

Come fa - thers and moth - ers, Come sis - ters and

mf legato

Come fa - thers and moth - ers, Come sis - ters and

mf legato

Come fa - thers and moth - ers, Come sis - ters and

mf legato

Come fa - thers and moth - ers, Come sis - ters and

27

upper voice legato

mf

31
broth - ers, Come join us in sing - ing the
broth - ers, Come join us in sing - ing the
broth - ers, Come join us in sing - ing the
broth - ers, Come join us in sing - ing the
31
Ped.
34
prais - es of Zi - on.
prais - es of Zi - on.
prais - es of Zi - on.
prais - es of Zi - on.
34
Ped.

37
37
40
mp
Come
mp
Come fa - thers and moth - ers, Come
mp
Come fa - thers and moth - ers, Come
mf
Come fa-thers and moth-ers, Come sis-ters and broth-ers, Come
40
mp (softly)
Ped.
Ped.
Ped.

43
sis - ters and broth - ers,
sis - ters and broth - ers,
join us in sing - ing the prais - es of Zi - on.
Ped. Ped. Ped. Ped.
45
O fa - thers don't you feel de - ter - mined to
O fa - thers don't you feel de - ter - mined to
to
to
Ped. Ped.

48
p sub.
meet_with-in__ the walls_ of Zi-on. We'll shout and go round,_
meet_with-in__ the walls_ of Zi-on. We'll shout and go round, we'll
div.
meet with-in the walls of Zi-on. We'll shout,___ we'll
meet with-in the walls of Zi-on. We'll shout,___ we'll
Ped.
51
crescendo
molto
shout and go round,_ shout and go round,_ shout and go round,_
shout and go round,_we'll shout and go round, we'll shout and go round_ the
shout,___ we'll shout,___ we'll shout,___ we'll
shout,___ we'll shout,___ we'll shout,___ we'll
Ped.

54
shout, the walls of Zi - on,
walls of Zi - on, the walls of Zi - on,
div.
unis.
shout, the walls of
shout, the walls of Zi - on, the walls of
Ped.
56
slightly slower
a tempo
div.
the walls of Zi - on.
the walls of Zi - on.
Zi - on, of Zi - on.
Zi - on, of Zi - on.
hold back
Ped.

3. THE GOLDEN WILLOW TREE

(Anglo-American Ballad)

Arranged by
AARON COPLAND
Transcribed for chorus by
GREGORY ROSE

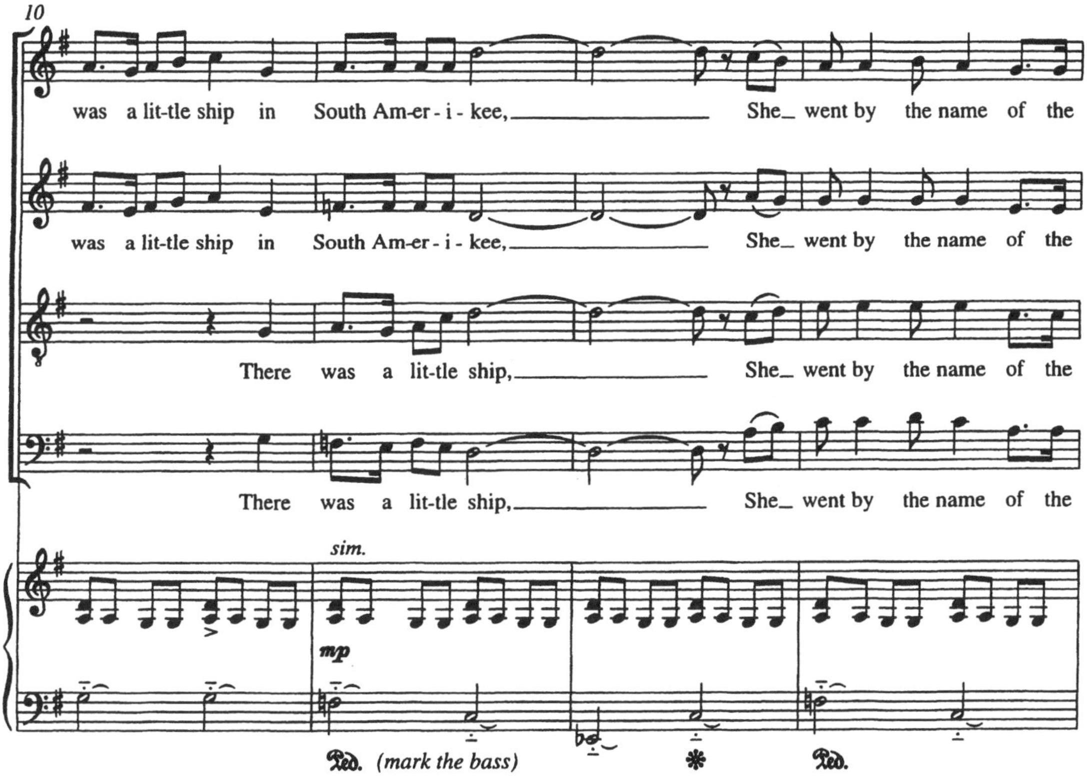

10

was a lit-tle ship in South Am-er-i-kee, She went by the name of the

was a lit-tle ship in South Am-er-i-kee, She went by the name of the

There was a lit-tle ship, She went by the name of the

There was a lit-tle ship, She went by the name of the

sim.

mp

Ped. *(mark the bass)* * Ped.

14
p
Gold-en Wil-low Tree, As she sailed,
p
Gold-en Wil-low Tree, As she sailed in the low land lone - some
Gold-en Wil-low Tree,
Gold-en Wil-low Tree,
p
17
As she sailed so low.
low, As she sailed in the low - land so low.
Ped.

20

mf

We hadn't been a-sail-in' more than two weeks or three, Till we

mf

We hadn't been a-sail-in' more than two weeks or three, Till we

mf

so low o so low so low o so low

mf

so low o so low so low o so low

(legato)

mp

Ped. Ped. Ped. *sim.*

23

came in sight of the Bri-tish Ro-ve-rie,

mp

As she sailed in the

came in sight of the Bri-tish Ro-ve-rie,

mp

As she sailed in the low -

so low o so low so low so low

so low o so low so low so low

p (misterioso)

26

low - land low, As she sailed in the low - land so

— land lone - some low, As she sailed in the low - land so

mp

As she sailed in the low - land so

29

mf *frank and open*

low. Up stepped a lit - tle

mf *frank and open*

low. Up stepped a lit - tle

low.

mp

(half stacc.)

32

car-pen-ter boy says

car-pen-ter boy says

mf

"What will you give me for the ship that I'll des-troy?"

mf

"What will you give me for the ship that I'll des-troy?"

35

(mf)

"I'll give gold

(mf)

"I'll give gold

f

"I'll give you gold or I'll give thee I'll

f

"I'll give you gold or I'll give thee I'll

(clouded)

mf

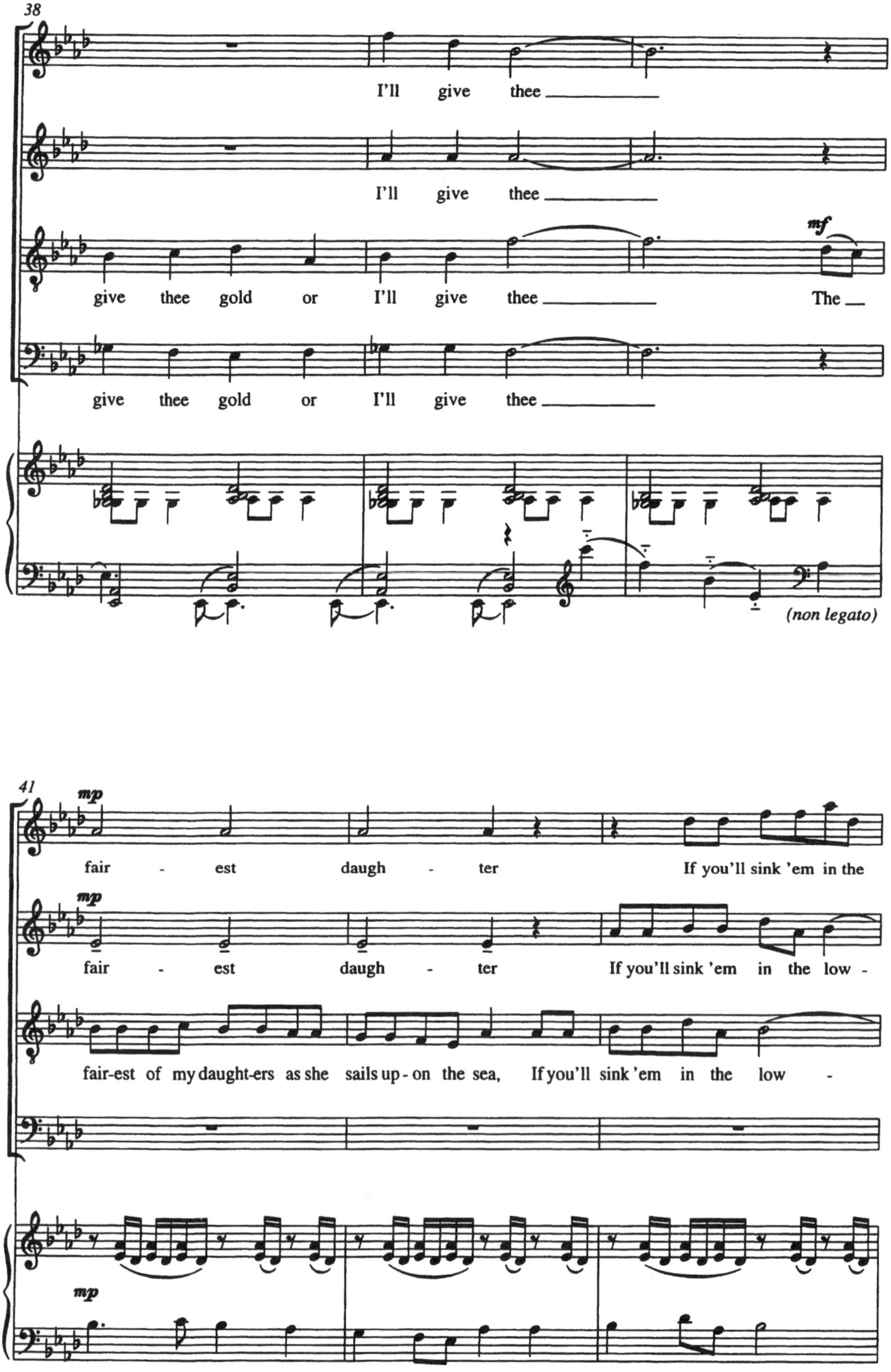

38

I'll give thee

I'll give thee

give thee gold or I'll give thee *mf* The

give thee gold or I'll give thee

(non legato)

44

low ______ If you'll

- land ______ If you'll sink 'em

__ land lone - some low, If you'll sink 'em in the

46

sink 'em in the land that lies so low." ______

in the land that lies so low." ______

land that lies so low." ______

f

49

p

He turned up-on his back and a -

p

He turned up-on his back and a -

p

He turned up-on his back and a -

p

He turned up-on his back and a -

(r.h. glassy)

p

52

way swum he, He — swum till he came to the Brit-ish Ro - ve - rie, He

way swum he, He swum till he came to the Brit-ish Ro - ve - rie, He

way swum he, He swum till he came to the Brit-ish Ro - ve - rie, He

way swum he, He swum till he came to the Brit-ish Ro - ve - rie, He

55

had a lit - tle in - stru - ment fit - ted for his use, He __ bored nine holes and he

had a lit - tle in - stru - ment fit - ted for his use, He bored nine holes and he

had a lit - tle in - stru - ment fit - ted for his use, He __ bored nine holes and he

had a lit - tle in - stru - ment fit - ted for his use, He bored nine holes and he

58

bored them all at once. He turned ________

bored them all at once. He turned ________

bored them all at once.

bored them all at once. He turned up - on his breast and back swum he, He __

61

he swum

he swum

swum till he came to the Gol - den Wil - low Tree.

63

mf

"Cap-tain Cap-tain Cap-tain Cap-tain Cap-tain Cap-tain

"Cap-tain Cap-tain Cap-tain Cap-tain Cap-tain Cap-tain

"Cap - tain, O cap-tain, come take me on board O cap - tain O cap-tain, come

"Cap-tain Cap-tain Cap-tain Cap-tain Cap-tain Cap-tain

mf

67

take me on board And do un - to me

take me on board And do un - to me

take me on board And do un - to me as good as your word. For I

on board And do un - to me

sub. **p**

71

(**p**)

I sank 'em in the

(**p**)

I sank 'em in the

sank 'em in the low - land lone - some low, I sank 'em in the

(**p**)

I sank 'em in the

74

low - land so low."

low - land so low."

low - land so low."

low - land so low."

ff

77

ff

"Oh no, I won't take

ff

"No, no

ff

"No, no

ff

"No, no

(strident)

sf *sf*

ff

80
you on board, Oh no, I won't take you on board, Nor _
no no, no _ no,
no no, no _ no,
no no, no _ no,
sf sf sf sf sf sf
83
mf
do un - to you as good as my word, Tho' you sank _
mf
do un - to you as good as my word, Tho' you sank _
mf
do un - to you as good as my word, Tho' you sank 'em in the low -
do un - to you as good as my word.
sf sf sf sf p sub.

86

sf

— low, Tho' you sank ______

sf

— low, Tho' you sank ______

sf

- land lone - some low, Tho' you sank 'em in the

88

— low." ______

— low." ______

land that lies so low." ______

non legato

f *(as at first)*

91
Tenor
p
"If it was-n't for the love that I
Bass
p
"If it was-n't for the love that I
(p)
94
have for your men, I'd do un-to you as I've done un-to them.
have for your men, I'd do un-to you as I've done un-to them, I'd sink you in the low -
(mp)
(poco accentuàto)
98
div.
- land lone - some low, I'd sink you in the low - land so

101 Soprano

down swum

Alto

p

He turned up-on his head and down swum he, ______

Tenor

Bass

low." ______

pp

(clouded)

105

he, ______

______

He turned up-on his head and

turned ______

unis.

turned ______

108
down swum he, He
down swum he, He
he,
he,
111
swum
swum till he came to the bot-tom of the sea. Sank him-
he swum
p

115
self — in the low - land lone - some low, sank him - self — in the
p
sank him - self — in the low.
pp
p
Ped. * Ped. * Ped. sim.
118
Alto
land that lies so low.
poco sf
mp
mf
121
(molto cresc.)
sff

4. AT THE RIVER

(Hymn Tune)

Arranged by
AARON COPLAND
Transcribed for chorus by
R. WILDING-WHITE

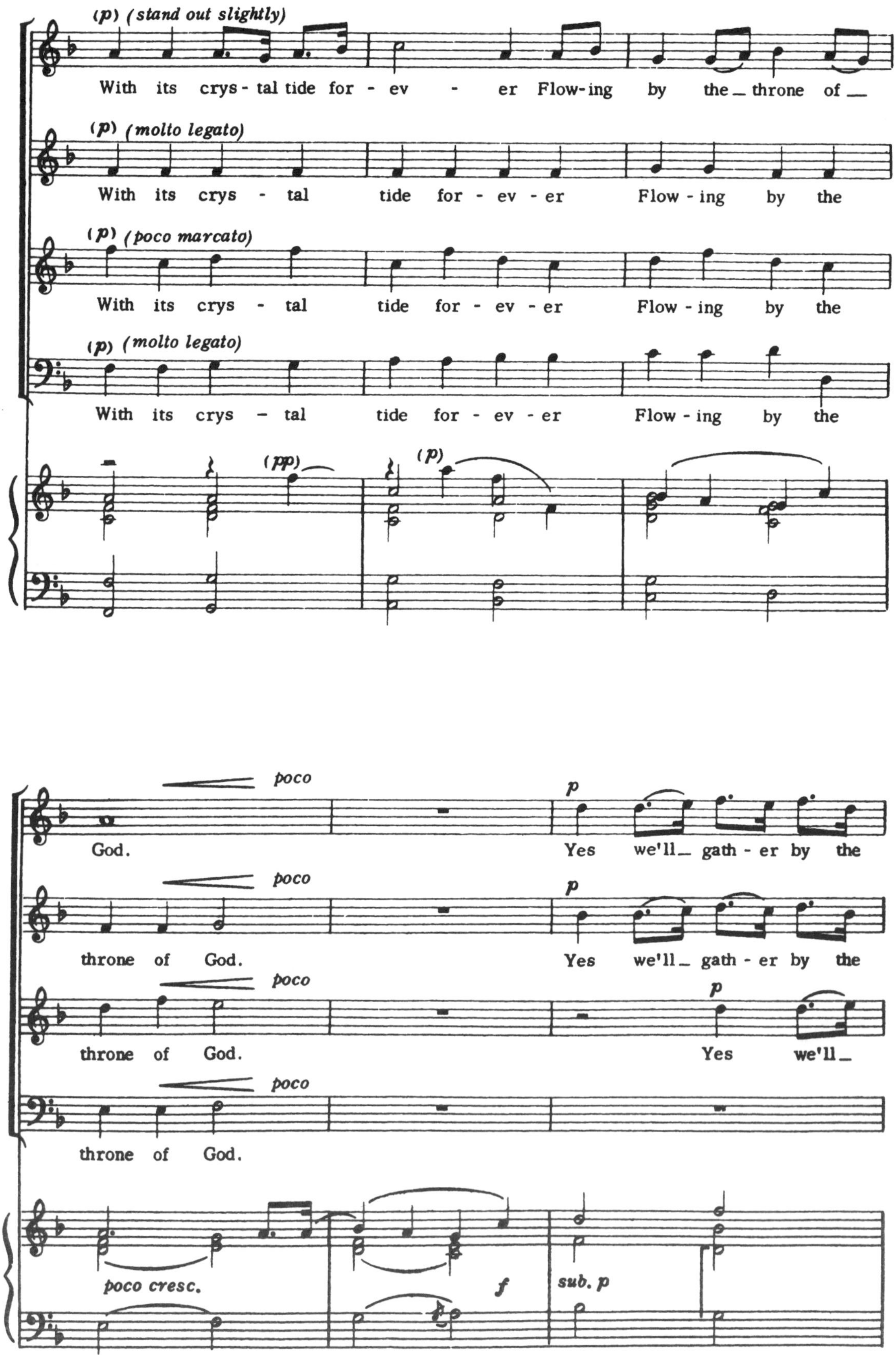

(p) (stand out slightly)

With its crys - tal tide for - ev - er Flow-ing by the _ throne of _

(p) (molto legato)

With its crys - tal tide for - ev - er Flow - ing by the

(p) (poco marcato)

With its crys - tal tide for - ev - er Flow - ing by the

(p) (molto legato)

With its crys - tal tide for - ev - er Flow - ing by the

(pp) *(p)*

riv - er, the beau - ti - ful, the beau - ti - ful
riv - er, the beau - ti - ful, the beau - ti - ful
gath - er by the riv - er, the beau - ti - ful, the beau - ti - ful
by the riv - er, by the riv - er,
riv - er, Gath - er with the saints by the riv - er That
riv - er, Gath - er with the saints by the riv - er That
riv - er, Gath - er with the saints by the riv - er That
by the riv - er, Gath - er with the saints by the riv - er That

Flows by the throne of God.
Flows by the throne of God.
Flows by the throne of God.
Flows by the throne of God.
cresc.
ff
Soon we'll reach the
ff
Soon we'll reach the shin - ing
ff
Soon we'll reach the
ff
Soon we'll
ff

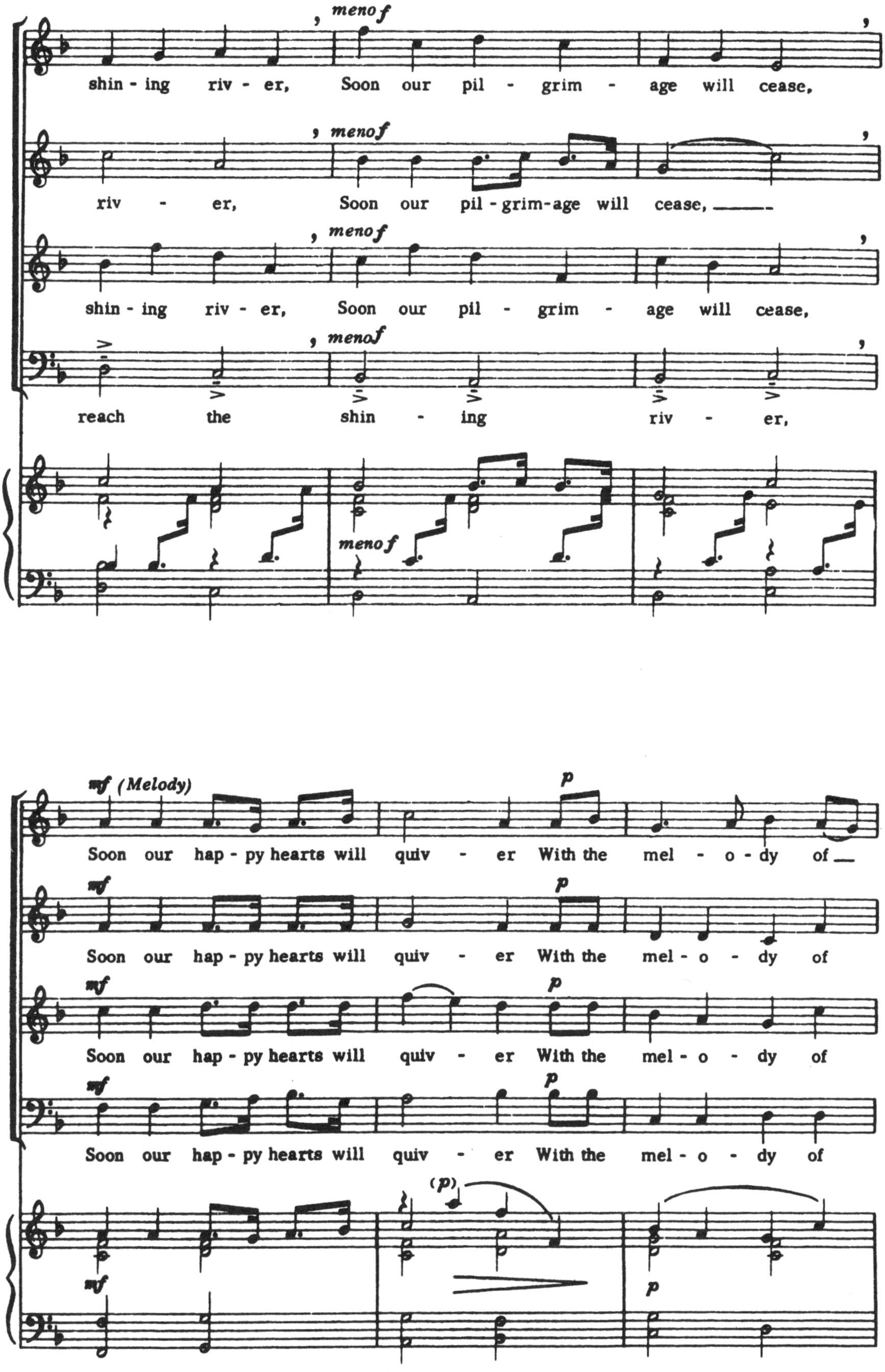

, meno f

shin - ing riv - er, Soon our pil - grim - age will cease,

, meno f

riv - er, Soon our pil - grim - age will cease,

, meno f

shin - ing riv - er, Soon our pil - grim - age will cease,

, meno f

reach the shin - ing riv - er,

meno f

poco

peace.

Yes we'll — gath - er by the

poco

peace. —

Yes we'll — gath - er by the

poco

peace. —

Yes we'll —

poco

peace. —

cresc.

(p)

f

sub. p

riv - er, the beau - ti - ful, the beau - ti - ful —

riv - er, the beau - ti - ful, the beau - ti - ful —

gath - er by the riv - er, the beau - ti - ful, the beau - ti - ful —

by the riv - er, the beau - ti - ful, the beau - ti - ful —

mf
riv - er, Gath - er with the saints_ by the riv - er That
riv - er, Gath - er with the saints_ by the riv - er That
riv - er, Gath - er with the saints_ by the riv - er That
riv - er, Gath - er with the saints by the riv - er That
cresc.
ff
rit.
flows by the throne of_ God, that flows by the throne of_ God.
flows by the throne of God, that flows by the throne of God.
flows by the throne of God, that_ flows by the throne of God.
flows by the throne of God, that flows by the throne of God.
mf cresc.
col 8..:

5. CHING-A-RING CHAW

(Minstrel Song)

Arranged by
AARON COPLAND
Transcribed for chorus by
IRVING FINE

Ho - a ding kum lar - kee.
Ho - a ding kum lar - kee.
Ho - a ding kum lar - kee.
Ho - a ding kum lar - kee.
mp
Broth - ers, Lis - ten to this sto - ry,
mp
Broth - ers, Lis - ten to this sto - ry,
mp
Broth-ers ga - ther round, Lis - ten to this sto - ry, 'Bout the
mp
Broth-ers ga - ther round, Lis - ten to this sto - ry, 'Bout the
mp

'Bout the prom-ised land, An' the prom-ised glo - ry.

'Bout the prom-ised land, An' the prom-ised glo - ry.

prom - ised, prom-ised land, An' the prom-ised glo - ry.

prom - ised, prom-ised land, An' the prom-ised glo - ry.

mp

Ching a-ring-a ring, Ching a-ring-a ring ching,

mp

Ching a-ring-a ring, Ching a-ring-a ring ching,

f

You don't need to fear

f

You don't need to fear

(banjo style)

f

Ching-a-ring-a ring, Ching-a-ring-a ring ching, Ching-a-ring-a ring,
Ching-a-ring-a ring, Ching-a-ring-a ring ching, Ching-a-ring-a ring,
If you have no mon-ey, You don't need none
If you have no mon-ey, You don't need none

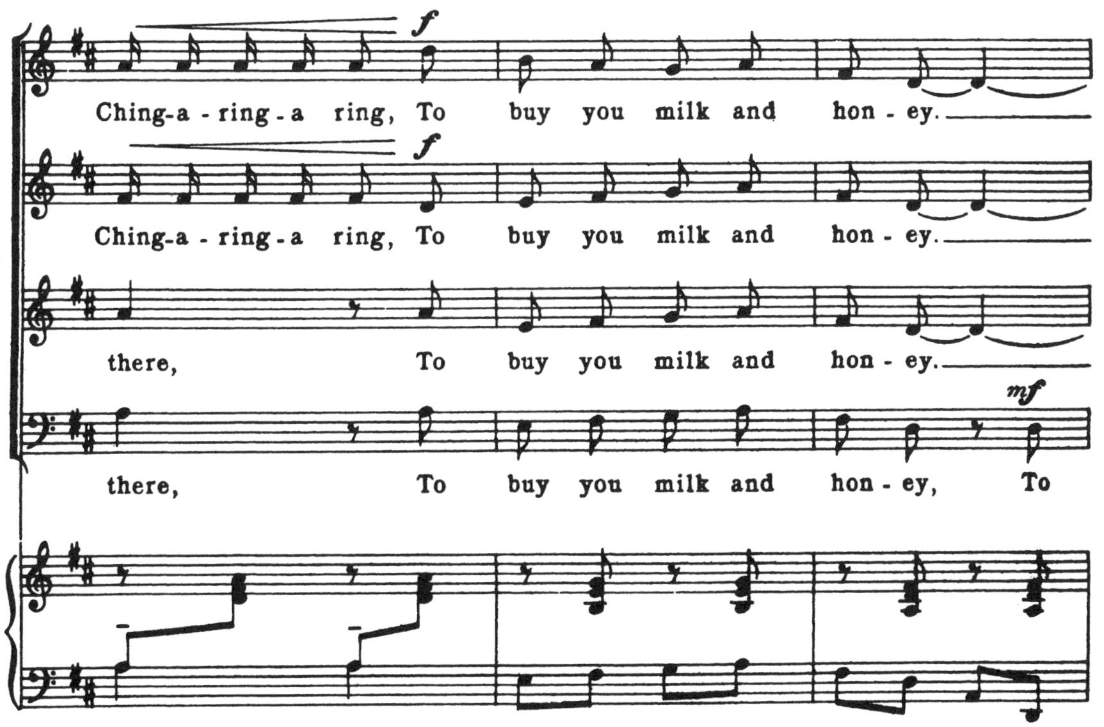
f
Ching-a-ring-a ring, To buy you milk and hon-ey.
f
Ching-a-ring-a ring, To buy you milk and hon-ey.
there, To buy you milk and hon-ey.
mf
there, To buy you milk and hon-ey, To

f

There you'll ride in

f

There you'll ride in

f

There you'll ride in

f

buy you milk and hon-ey. There you'll ride in

mp

f

p
one, two, three, four cours-es.
Ching-a-ring-a ring ching
one, two, three, four cours-es.
p
one, two, three, four cours-es.
Ching-a-ring-a
one, two, three, four cours-es.
mp
ching,
Ho-a ding-a ding kum
p
Ching-a-ring-a ring ching
ching,
Ho-a ding-a
ring ching ching,
Ho-a ding-a ding kum
p
Ching-a-ring-a ring,
Ho-a ding-a

mp mp mp mp

lar - kee. Ching-a - ring-a ring ching, Ho- a ding kum

ding kum lar - kee. Ching-a - ring-a ring ching, Ho - a ding kum

lar - kee. Ching-a - ring-a ring ching, Ho - a ding kum

ding kum lar - kee. Ching-a - ring-a ring ching, Ho - a ding kum

mf f mf f sf

lar - kee. We will

lar - kee. Nights we all will dance,

lar - kee. Nights we will

lar - kee.

dance, To the harp, Jig and
To the harp and fid-dle, Waltz and jig and prance,
dance, To the harp, Jig and
"Cast off down the mid-dle."
"Cast off down the mid-dle."
prance.

ff
When the morn-in' come, All in grand and splen-dor,
ff
When the morn-in' come, All in grand and splen-dor,
ff
When the morn-in' come, All in grand and splen-dor,
ff
When the morn-in' come, All in grand and splen-dor,
8
ff (jubilant)
Ped.
Ped.
Stand out in the sun, And hear the ho - ly thun-der.
Stand out in the sun, And hear the ho - ly thun-der.
Stand out in the sun, And hear the ho - ly thun-der.
Stand out in the sun, And hear the ho - ly thun-der.
sf
Ped.
Ped.
Ped.

8
sf
sf
sf
molto sf
sub. p
Ped.
Ped.
mf
Broth-ers, The
mf
Broth-ers, The
mf
Broth-ers hear me out, The
mf
Broth-ers hear me out, The
mf

f
prom - ised land's a-come-in', Dance, sing and shout, I
f
prom - ised land's a-come-in', Dance and sing and shout, I
f
prom-ised land's a - come - in', Dance and sing and shout, I
f
prom-ised land's a - come - in', Dance and sing and shout, I
f
ff
hear them harps a - strum-min'.(n)
ff
hear them harps a - strum-min'.(n)
ff
hear them harps a - strum-min'.(n)
ff
hear them harps a - strum-min'.(n)
ff

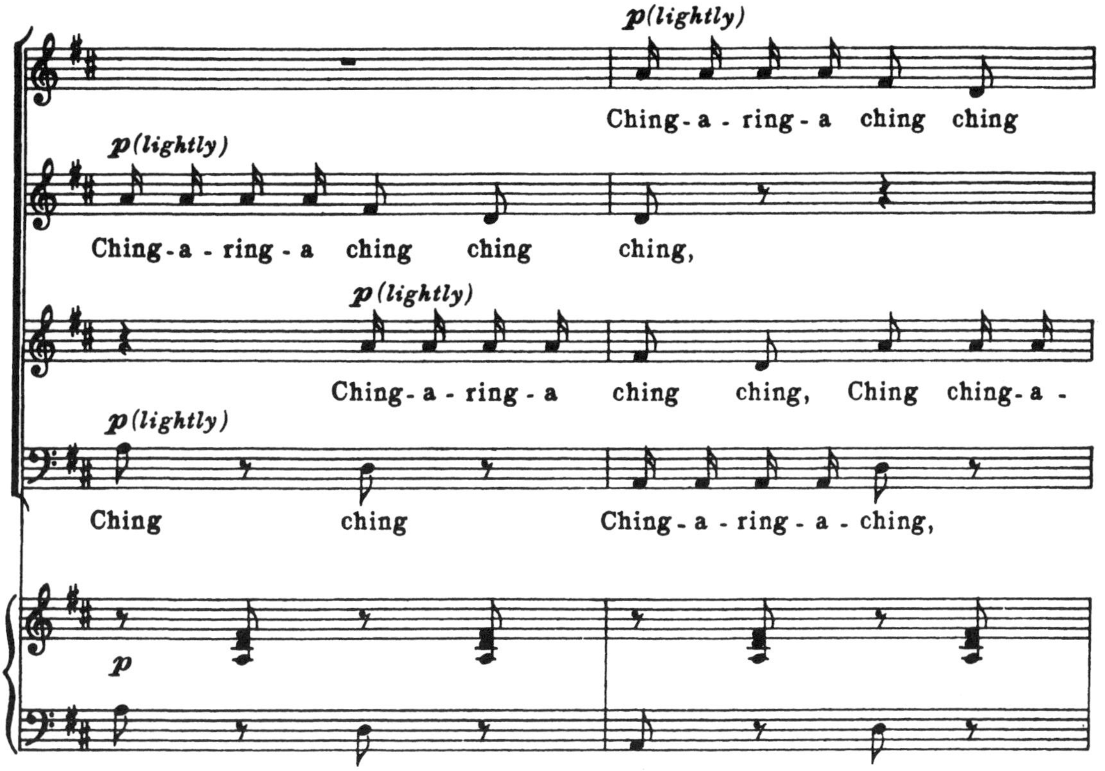
p(lightly)
Ching-a-ring-a ching ching
p(lightly)
Ching-a-ring-a ching ching ching,
p(lightly)
Ching-a-ring-a ching ching, Ching ching-a-
p(lightly)
Ching ching Ching-a-ring-a-ching,
p

ching, Ching ching-a-ring ching ching-a-ching,
Ching-a-ring-a ching ching ching ching,
ring ching ching-a-ching, Ching-a-ring-a
Ching ching, Ching-a-ring-a ching,

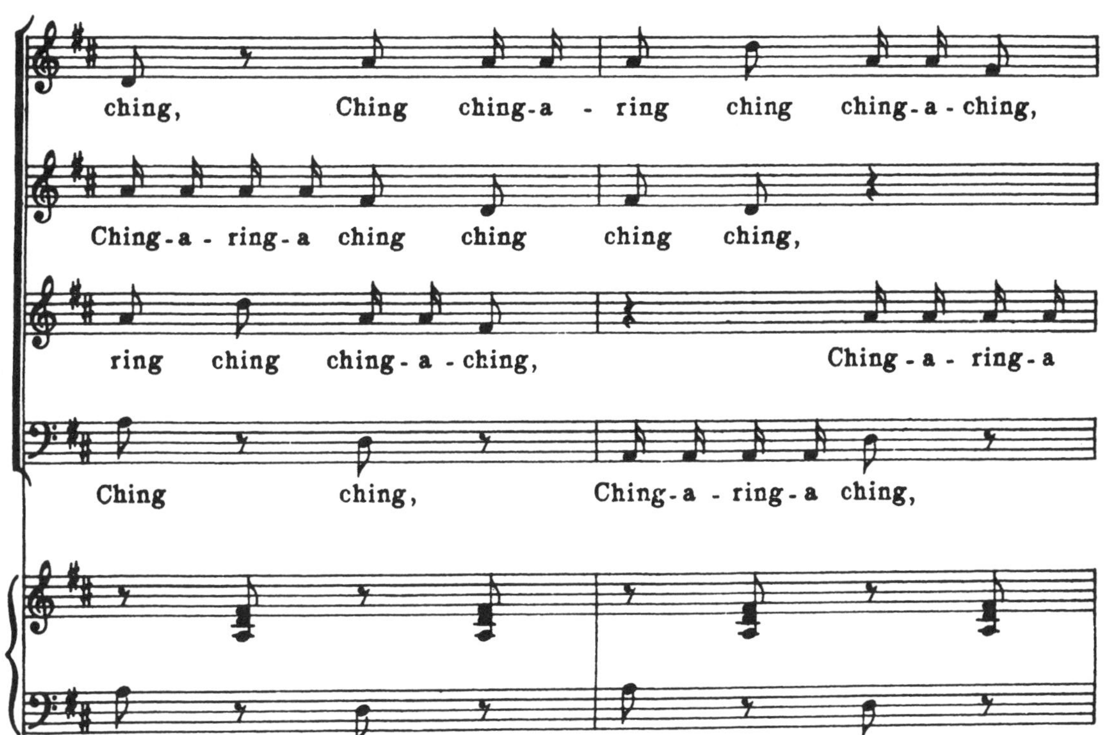

cresc.
Ching-a-ring-a ching ching, Ching-a-ring-a ching ching, Ching-a-ring-a
cresc.
Ching-a-ring-a ching ching, Ching-a-ring-a ching ching, Ching-a-ring-a
cresc.
ching ching-a ching ching-a ching ching ching ching, Ching-a-ring-a
cresc.
Ching ching, Ching-a-ring-a ching, Ching-a-ring-a
ff (shouted)
ching-a-ring-a ching-a-ring-a, Ring ching ching ching Chaw!
ff (shouted)
ching-a-ring-a ching-a-ring-a, Ring ching ching ching Chaw!
ff (shouted)
ching-a-ring-a ching-a-ring-a, Ring ching ching ching Chaw!
ff (shouted)
ching-a-ring-a ching-a-ring-a, Ring ching ching ching Chaw!
8
sff